The
Fife Canary

Terry Kelly

Dedication

This book is dedicated to
Janet Turnbull
who, in life and in death,
was an inspiration to us all.

Acknowledgements

I should like to thank:

Andy McEwan for producing the paintings of Fifes

John E Haith, Seed Merchants, for sponsoring the paintings

Gilli Milner for typing the manuscript

Pam for her support

Contents

Introduction

On a cold Wednesday afternoon in March 1959, while I was still a pupil at Batley Grammar School, I went to Dewsbury market to collect my first pair of Bullfinches for the princely sum of £2, saved from my pocket money. Bullfinches were the birds of my dreams and to this day I enjoy their occasional visits to my garden. Thus began a lifelong love of aviculture. To own, breed and care for my own birds was to prove an irresistible challenge that I still find exciting to this day.

I did not exhibit a bird for 20 years. My love was breeding native species in natural conditions, moving from hardbills such as the the Bullfinch to softbills such as the Redstart and Grey Wagtail. Along the way I flirted with different types of canary (my grandfather had kept Borders) and I moved on to them entirely when I discovered the gem of all canaries: the Fife.

Over 30 years ago I read a quote from a leading fancier in the avicultural magazine *Cage & Aviary Birds* in which he reminded readers that foreign birdkeeping was the fastest growing section of aviculture in Britain: *Sooner or later the newcomer to foreign birds realises he wants the 'perfect bird' – a seedeater with no need for livefood, peaceful, attractive and beautiful... must have a lovely song, must breed readily and without traumatic complications and is not expensive.* He came to the conclusion that the only bird that satisfied all of these requirements was a canary.

The Fife canary more than any other meets these requirements today. It comes in a wide variety of colours and is now well established as the most popular breed of canary in the United Kingdom and in many other parts of the world.

I like to feel I have played a part in this meteoric rise in popularity. When I started keeping birds in 1959 the Fife canary was not even in existence. Over the last 20 years I have bred over 3,000 Fife canaries which have been distributed throughout the world, thus enabling other fanciers to achieve great success. I have won every major Fife show in the country and, in the late 1980s, when I probably had the finest stud of Fife canaries in the world, won all the major honours at the National Exhibition of Cage and Aviary Birds held in Birmingham. I am now Chairman of the North of England Fife Fancy Canary Club and was its Secretary for many of its formative years. In this time I helped to turn it into the largest Fife club in the world, with the largest specialist Fife show held each year on the penultimate Sunday of November. I have also encouraged the popularity of the Fife canary in my regular articles in *Cage & Aviary Birds* and in a book I co-authored in 1988.

Over the past 10 years the Fife's popularity has increased many fold and the top exhibits have improved beyond recognition. For this reason I have chosen to give the Fife canary the recognition it now deserves by writing this book which hopefully will help exhibitors and newcomers alike in this most wonderful of hobbies.

The author with his Supreme Winner at the National Exhibition of Cage and Aviary Birds, 1987.

Chapter

One History of the Fife Canary

The First Pet Canaries

Old books about the canary carry many diverse accounts of how the wild canary came into Britain. What is perfectly clear is that it has been here for over 400 years and has had a similar spread and rise in popularity across the world, becoming the most popular songbird in aviculture.

The wild canary, a species of the *Serin* finch genus, was found only on the islands off the West coast of Africa: the Canary Islands, Madeira, Azores and Cape Verde Islands in particular. Its habitat was dense vegetation on steep slopes and it was able to produce several rounds of young each year in the mild climate.

The original Spanish settlers and seamen were attracted initially to the birds' song, as their plumage was relatively dull. According to old drawings the original canary was self buff green in colour with dark brown shading, but it had the markings found in all the serin/siskin type finches. Many wild canaries were caught and taken back to Spain, where their song quickly established them as popular pets. Very soon nearly every well-to-do household boasted its own singing canary.

There are many other romantic stories telling how the canary arrived in Europe. One of the most famous is that, when a ship was wrecked off the coast of Elba, some canaries escaped from it. They were then transported to Italy where they became popular, spreading from there across Europe. However, it is more likely that the canaries arrived by a variety of routes, as seamen calling at Madeira and other islands would take them on board as pets. It is very likely that the indigenous people had already established them as songbird pets. Ships from France, Spain and Portugal visited those islands regularly, to trade as well as to occupy and rule.

One of the author's hen Siskins. Of similar size to the Fife, it makes an ideal aviary companion and hybridises readily.

The Development of Varieties

The early German fanciers developed the canary's song to the level it is today, when it rivals the Nightingale and Blackbird. Although a small bird, a cock canary in full breeding condition can equal any other songbird in power.

The German fanciers also developed the specialised song of the Roller canary. These birds were known as Hartz Mountain Rollers in my grandfather's day, as the original birds were developed in that area of Germany. Even today it is the only variety of canary bred for its song and singing competitions are still held for this particular breed. All other breeds of canary are bred for their colour, shape, size and feather quality and occasionally for special markings in such varieties as the Gloster and Lizard. New varieties are still being formed – the Stafford was produced in the 1990s from a combination of other breeds.

The earliest recorded domesticated variety of canary is probably the Lizard, which dates back to the early 18th century. Bred for its variety of colour and markings, it is still very popular.

The Norwich (often referred to as the *Norwich Plainhead* to distinguish it from the *Crested Norwich* which is now extinct) was also produced in the 18th century, around the area of Norwich, and this too remains very popular. It has changed little in shape over the past 200 years.

Other types of canary were produced in the early 1800s, including some of the 'frilled' (curly-feathered) and slimmer varieties such as the Belgium, Scottish, Frilled, Lancashire and Old Dutch.

The Yorkshire Canary was produced in that county towards the end of the last century and this was a very slim bird that has changed little in shape for the past 100 years. My grandfather when describing an ideal Yorkshire canary would say, "It would have slipped through a wedding ring!"

However, the newer varieties are by far the most popular now. The Border, Gloster and Fife dominate the major shows in the United Kingdom, particularly the National Exhibition of Cage and Aviary Birds held at the National Exhibition Centre, Birmingham each year during the first weekend in December.

The Coloured Canary is another new breed and, though not as popular as the three identified above, is still very popular. This is particularly so in Europe where the range of colours and shades increases year by year.

The Development of the Fife Canary

Border Canary

To understand the history of the Fife canary we must look at the development of the Border Canary from the middle of the last century up to the early post-war period. It is since then that the canary with a Border/Fife shape has developed. Even half a century ago the Border and Fife were one breed. Since that time they have gone their separate ways in size while retaining many of the same characteristics and qualities, much as Toy and Miniature Poodles have.

The Border Fancy Canary was formed in the middle of the 19th century in the county of Cumberland while the Yorkshire was being developed a couple of hundred miles further south. The Border Fancy was known as the Cumberland Fancy in parts of the country and, as its popularity increased, it spread northwards to the borders of Scotland where it also became the most popular breed of canary.

A meeting was called in July 1890, and from this historic event in Hawick was born the official Border Fancy Canary Club (BFCC). In the following year came the very first model of the Border Fancy Canary, based on a bird owned by a Mr McMillan of Langholm.

The meeting had come about because of a quarrel between fanciers in the counties of Cumberland, Dumfries, Roxburgh and Selkirk. At the centre of the quarrel was the fact that fanciers in Cumberland had decided to call their local canary the Cumberland Fancy. Fanciers in the other three counties took exception to this, claiming that the bird had originally evolved in Scotland's border counties.

Good sense seems to have prevailed in the first place – hence the meeting in Hawick. But all was not well. The meeting was attended mostly by Scottish fanciers who took control of the newly created BFCC. One outcome of this was that for nearly 15 years the Border grew in popularity in Scotland but made no progress in England and Wales. It was not until the English and Welsh BFCC was formed in 1905 that the Border's popularity rapidly increased throughout the United Kingdom.

The bird of that period bore no resemblance to the present-day Border and very little to the present-day Fife, although it was closer in shape and size to the smaller breed. The bird was relatively small with very little rise on the back and less leg, which meant it did not have the freedom of movement of modern birds.

Photographs of winning Border canaries in the 1950s and 1960s show a bird very similar to today's Fife; indeed, fanciers returning to the fancy after a lapse of 30 years consider today's Fife to be nearer to the birds they used to breed than today's Border.

Today's Borders are far larger than the birds of yesterday. Even winning Borders of the 1970s and 1980s appear smaller and much slimmer than the show winners of today.

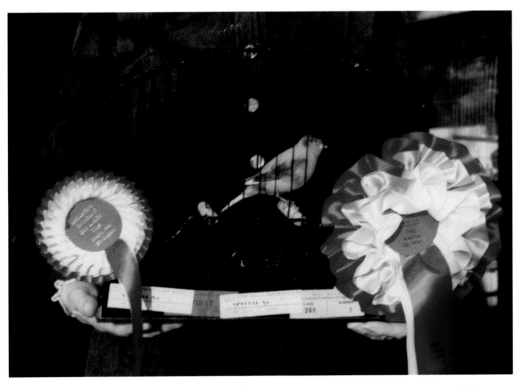

The author's winner of the Haith Trophy 1982 for best Adult Canary at the National Exhibition.
(Excellent colour, but modern Fifes have better type.)

A National Exhibition winning Green Fife hen (1995) bred by A F Weaver. Photo: Dennis Avon

The Fife as an individual breed

It was the increase in size of the Border that led to the creation of the Fife as an individual breed. Fanciers north of the Border, feeling that the 'wee gem' was becoming too large and that winning birds did not reflect the true model, tried to reverse the trend by breeding the bird back to its original size. Several leading Scottish fanciers today have studs developed from those Borders of the 1950s, but they have line-bred downwards in size rather than upwards.

During recent years fanciers have noticed the developing interest in the Fife and it is now the most popular canary. Yet it was virtually unheard of 35 years ago. It first appeared as a variety in 1952. The breed was developing and growing in popularity in the region of Fife in Scotland, so it was named by those fanciers. Even today this area remains one of the strongholds of the breed. Not only is it one of the youngest breeds of canary – it is also the smallest, the ideal being 11cm or 4¼in (although it must be said that only a yellow-feathered hen could achieve this dimension).

The Fife was relatively slow to catch on outside Fife initially, but people who saw it were impressed with its jauntiness, type and feather texture. In England classes were provided for 'miniature Borders' but these were not taken seriously until the late 1970s.

Perhaps the most famous Fife canary ever exhibited was the self fawn shown by Walter Lumsden in the Any Other Variety (AOV) Canary Class at the National Exhibition of Cage and

Aviary Birds in 1973. Walter was the founder member of the Fife Fancy Canary Club (FFCC), which was formed in 1957, and most years he can be seen at the annual National Exhibition in his tartan kilt. This particular bird went on to become the Best Canary at the exhibition.

Fifes were given their own classes in 1975 when 50 birds were exhibited. Today a minimum of 1,500 Fifes is exhibited – more than any other variety.

Some of the earliest members of the FFCC still compete at the highest levels each year without ever having introduced new blood into their studs.

My own introduction to Fifes was in the 1970s when I visited my friend of many years, Tom Patterson, a Scottish miner who had settled in South Yorkshire. Tom had just returned from Scotland with some Fife Canaries to use as foster parents for his British birds. He referred to them as *Scottish Borders* at that time. These active, colourful little creatures really caught my eye and I have been hooked on them ever since.

Increasing in popularity

By then the Fife was becoming popular south of the Border. Keith Mackintosh was a forerunner with the breed in Wales, David Myton in Northern England and Sid Stratton in Southern England.

A Clear Yellow hen in the late 1980s. She was a quality bird for her time, but 10 years of selective breeding have improved the 'type' or roundness.

The North of England FFCC became the first club to be formed outside Scotland and others have sprung up across the country over the past 20 years, reflecting the breed's increasing popularity. The Fife Fancy Federation was formed in 1983 from the then seven major Fife clubs as the governing body. A list of specialist Fife clubs can be found on page 111.

As the variety has gone from strength to strength in numbers, the standard of the top exhibition birds has improved in both type and quality. Fifes are now doing well against other canary breeds at shows and often take Best Canary in Show awards. The numbers are still increasing too, whereas in many of the other breeds numbers are decreasing. In most areas of the country the Fife entry now exceeds the Border in number and the rate of increase shows no sign of slowing down.

The largest Fife canary show in the country is the North of England FFCC Club Show, held each year on the penultimate Sunday in November in West Yorkshire. Over 1,200 birds are now entered each year and it is only a question of time before there is an entry of 2,000 birds at a major Fife show.

The many reasons for its popularity compared with other canary breeds include:

- *Variety of colours available* Fifes are available in both buff and yellow feather types (see definitions in chapter 5) with a far greater depth of colour than almost all other varieties. Good quality clear, greens, cinnamons, whites, blues, fawns and variegated birds with different colours are available.

- *Feather quality* Other breeds have lost out in feather quality by introducing different varieties into the existing blood. The Fife's feather quality is superb in the top exhibits and is an important part of the exhibition Fife. This is probably due to top breeders always pairing yellows to buffs (see chapter 5).

- *Good breeders* Although not quite as prolific as they were 20 years ago, today's Fifes remain good breeders and the adults are usually very good parents. Many varieties such as the Norwich and Border now appear to be sluggish rearers whereas 20 pairs of Fifes rear up to 100 youngsters with very little trouble. They also produce young whether in the warm Mediterranean countries or the very remote Highlands of Scotland.

- *Inexpensive to buy* Bird fanciers spend a relative fortune on some foreign birds, which also need expensive heating equipment. Others spend vast sums on a British hybrid that cannot breed. Even some varieties of canary, particularly the Border these days, can be expensive, but top class Fifes are still available at very reasonable prices. Do not be tempted to buy cheap birds but go to a top breeder who will sell you quality youngsters at a fair price.

A further reason for its popularity is that the Dewar show cage (see chapter 10) is used to exhibit both Fifes and Borders. Fanciers can move easily from one breed to the other and many leading exhibitors, including the author, keep both varieties because of this mutual show cage.

Whereas other breeds have become more sluggish with the increase in size, or their feather texture has become coarse, the Fife always appears active and inquisitive as soon as it is weaned. This is noticed particularly by breeders who keep them alongside Borders or Glosters.

To conclude...

The Fife fancy canary has seen a dramatic increase in popularity over the past 10 years and hopefully will continue to do so. Fanciers who keep British birds or other breeds of canary admit to being attracted to them at shows. They are certainly eye-catching, with their jauntiness and colour. There is a great challenge in breeding so small a bird with type – yet more first class birds are now being exhibited. Maybe the men of Fife were right in rejecting the larger breed in favour of their 'marble on an egg'.

Chapter
Two Housing

Most Fife canaries are kept in wire cages as household pets, in an aviary collection or in a birdroom as part of a serious breeding programme.

Cock Fife canaries make ideal household pets because of their diminutive size and they are quite at home in all-wire budgerigar-type cages. They should not be given any toys but should be provided with two perches as far apart as possible so they can have good movement within the cage. They should be kept only one to a cage.

Canaries make a colourful display in an outdoor aviary. An aviary is an outdoor enclosure, usually made of wood covered with wire mesh. I shall describe its structure in more detail later in this chapter. Their song makes them ideal aviary inmates and they are unlikely to be aggressive with other species of birds. Always have more hens than cocks to keep any squabbling in spring to a minimum. One disadvantage is that birds are liable to get dirty when kept in an aviary.

A birdroom is a solid construction, usually wooden, in which birds are housed within cages rather than having the free flying facility they enjoy in an aviary. Most Fife canaries are kept in birdrooms, with each bird having an individual cage for much of the year. Being tough little birds, Fifes can be housed outdoors in a shed or brick-build birdroom all winter. I have a stone building with double glazing so that the water will not freeze in winter and the birdhouse will not get over-heated during the hot summer months. Alternatively, the cages can be accommodated in a spare bedroom in the house. The room should not be allowed to become too warm and the electric light should not be left on too frequently, as these have the effect of bringing the birds into false breeding condition.

Cages should be of the normal double breeder design, not less than 82cm (32in) in length 30cm (12in) high and 20–25cm (8–10in) deep. Double breeders have been described as 'orange boxes' as they are essentially wooden boxes divided into two with a wooden partition (to separate the cock from the hen at various times) and a wire cage front. Treble breeders would be of similar construction, but larger, and able to be divided into three for a cock and two hens.

If Fifes are purchased in the autumn it is as well to keep the cocks separate from the hens over the winter period so that the hens can be conditioned and prepared for the following breeding season.

Adjoining external aviaries can be used to good effect provided that all necessary precautions have been taken to prevent vermin from burrowing under the main frames and cats from causing mischief on the sides and the roof, particularly at night. They can be used for the hens in winter to keep them fit and slim ready for breeding in the spring and for the youngsters.

The most important requirements for Fifes are good ventilation and good lighting.

Outdoor Aviaries

Canaries can live outdoors all year round, even surviving very low temperatures. I have had them winter outdoors; when the ice on their water dishes has been broken they will immediately bathe, even before sunrise. In such an environment they will build a nest in natural trees as early as February in an attempt to breed, even if there is snow on the floor of their enclosure.

A 'planted' outdoor aviary, suitable for canaries and small finches.

Size of aviary
Much will depend on the space available. Most gardens have a site which lends itself to the construction of an aviary – either behind a garage or against a boundary wall. A rough guide for space is to allocate 2m depth by 1m width and 2m height (6ft x 3ft x 6ft) for one cock and two hens.

Construction
An outdoor aviary or 'flight' needs:

* a solid structure and foundation
* some protection from the elements mainly for feeding points
* protection from predators and small rodents
* an attractive outlook

The main wooden spars should be at least 5cm x 5cm (2in x 2in) square (or you could use strong rustic poles) and the whole structure should be covered by 1.75cm (⅝in) gauge galvanised mesh. This is available covered in green plastic, which makes maintenance very easy and is more of a deterrent to mice. Ordinary galvanised mesh should be painted black to make it easier to see the birds and to stop the mesh from rotting.

At least half the roof should be covered by perspex sheets to allow maximum daylight while keeping rain off the roosting and feeding points. The sides and front can be left open and shrubs and climbing plants encouraged to grow up the main spars, thus blending the aviary into the garden.

Floor and plants

A concrete floor has the advantage of being vermin-proof and easily washed down. A soil floor is better in larger aviaries as it allows the planting of evergreen shrubs such as laurel, which is cheap to buy, very tough and grows well, providing roosting places as well as a green outlook all year. Deciduous shrubs and privet are unsuitable as the birds virtually destroy them by continually nibbling any new shoots. Conifers look well but are best planted in pots so that they can be removed after a while and allowed to recover from the attentions of the birds.

Plants such as clematis and ivy can be grown on the outside and up the main spars and look extremely attractive. Hops too can be grown and have the advantage of attracting insects. Russian vine can be grown over the top of the aviary, thus providing a natural setting, attracting small insects (which will drop into the aviary and be eaten by the canaries) and making it difficult for cats to run around the top and frighten the birds. However, this plant can become very heavy after a few years.

Deterring predators

Cats will kill birds that roost at the side of the mesh at night, so ensure that roosting perches do not touch the outer mesh. Cats will also scare nesting birds off their nests, particularly at night. The only cure is a false roof made from a material such as poultry mesh one foot off the main roof so that they cannot run on it.

Rats can be a problem, as they will burrow under the main spars running along the ground and, once inside, will kill every bird. A simple solution is to run the 1.75cm (⅝in) gauge mesh down about 30cm (12in) below the level of the ground and 30cm (12in) outwards. Broken glass is then used to fill in the hole before the soil is put back. Any rat digging down will soon be deterred.

Weasels are efficient killers and can squeeze through a hole big enough for a large mouse. The mesh will keep them out, but any gaps or breakages must be repaired. Several leading fanciers I have known have had their entire stock wiped out by these predators, mainly by carelessness on the owner's part.

Mice will enter the aviary sooner or later and, if not checked, will become well established. The main food area should be suspended from the ceiling or positioned on top of a pole so that the mice cannot access it. However, they will still eat the seed that inevitably will be spilt and contaminate it. The best defence is to set three mouse traps under a wooden inverted seed tray with a weight placed on top so that it cannot be blown over. Check the traps every weekend and change the bait, using either cheese or chocolate. Any mouse gaining access to the aviary will burrow under the seed tray and be caught.

Perches

Natural perches look best, placed around the aviary. Always place them at head height, one at each end, thus encouraging the birds to fly the full length of the aviary and gain maximum exercise, particularly in the build-up to the breeding season.

Drinking water
I have found an inverted dustbin lid or something similar set into the soil ideal for drinking and bathing. If the water freezes in winter the lid is easier to empty than a solid earthenware dish because it is flexible. Do not supply water in deep dishes as young birds are likely to drown in it.

Pathways
The final touch is to place flags or stepping stones in the soil leading to the main feeding and drinking points; otherwise the soil will turn to mud in winter.

Birdrooms
Most Fife canary breeders and exhibitors have an outdoor birdroom. Many of these are solid wood structures but some are converted garages or an integral part of the house.

My current one is built of stone to match the bungalow but I have had a brick one built on the side of the house in the past. Both are solid birdrooms and do not have the disadvantages of a wooden structure.

The author's stone-built birdroom (20ft by 10ft or 6.1m by 3.1m).

Wooden structures need more maintenance and are not as vermin-proof. One fancier friend lost all his birds to a rat that climbed to the top of his shed and found a rotting corner at one end. Wooden structures are also colder in the winter months and any attempt at insulation appears to provide mice with a safe retreat.

If you are building a wooden birdroom or converting an existing shed ensure that rain water runs off the roof to prevent any damp areas causing future problems. Most important of all: raise the structure well off the floor.

Light and ventilation
Lighting and ventilation are the two most important features of any birdroom. You need sufficient light in the birdroom without causing a greenhouse effect in the summer.

The back of the birdroom should be solid so that cages can be stacked along the entire length. The front should have as much window space as possible. Wherever possible the windows should face east or south-east. Try to avoid windows facing south-west or west as they will attract the full day's sun in summer, which will prove too much for the birds. Incubating hens and youngsters in the nest are very uncomfortable under these conditions.

Several years ago I pulled down my purpose-built stone birdroom which was too exposed to the midday sun and

Birdroom (side view), showing ample light and breeding cages.

rebuilt it to face east. The birds were clearly uncomfortable and in many cases came into early moult. I had made the mistake when I moved into the property of using an existing greenhouse base on which to build my birdroom. The birds now get the mild early morning sun, which they clearly enjoy, and by midday the sun is shining on to the side wall.

Fresh air is essential, but cover the windows with very small gauge metal mesh (¼ in) to keep out predators such as weasels and mice.

Roy Fox of Wisbech, my friend and fellow fancier, has solid sides to his birdroom and has built-in roof light panels in preference to windows. This gives him more cage space and he feels the birds are not subjected to car lights, neighbours' security lights and so on, which might startle them.

Some fanciers use patterned glass to allow light through while minimising any sudden frights to the birds.

The birdroom must have good ventilation. Most fanciers leave windows open all year. However, these must always be covered with a small gauge mesh to keep out vermin and predators.

Whilst windows are being put in it is a good idea also to have a burglar alarm fitted to the doors and windows, particularly if there is an existing alarm system for the house.

Water

A healthy, clean birdroom requires quantities of water, and the installation of running water makes for a smoother operation. When I rebuilt my birdroom I installed an automatic dishwasher as I had additional space. This might seem a little over the top but it saves invaluable time in a busy daily schedule. A small water heater is used to boil small amounts of water in the winter months.

Electricity
Electricity is another essential in the modern birdroom. As well as providing lighting it offers the opportunity to install many of the essential modern appliances described later in the chapter.

Floor
Concrete floors covered with lino are ideal. One fancier I know has carpet as a floor covering and vacuums every day. Remember that seed, water, wood shavings and so on will fall on to the floor daily, so the floor will need to be swept and kept dry.

Concrete floors have a reputation for being cold but I do not find them so when covered with lino. Similarly, lino is a good covering material in a wooden shed raised off the ground.

Cages
The Fife fancy canary fancier will need six types of cages:

- *Breeding cages* These are of the wooden box type with a wire front, two perches and a feeding and drinking point.
- *Flight cages* These are long cages, usually 2m (6ft) or more in length, for wintering stock or housing youngsters during the summer. Most fanciers use partitions to divide these into four or five breeding cages.
- *Show cages* These are used to exhibit Fifes at shows. The model currently known as the Dewar show cage is described in chapter 10.
- *Weaning cages* These are small cages used for a few days only to wean the youngsters away from their mother before they are transferred to a flight cage (see chapter 7).
- *Training cages* These are used to condition Fifes for showing. They are hung on to the flight cages and are often old show cages (see chapter 8).
- *Hospital cages* These are used to house sick birds (see chapter 13). However, I normally use training cages placed in warm spots for this purpose.

Making breeding cages
I like my breeding cages to get the early morning sun, so I position them opposite the windows. That way the birds will reach breeding condition at the right time.

Breeding cages are easy to make and the size of the birdroom may determine the size of the cages. Do not have them too small, but too large is unnecessary and a waste of useful space.

I prefer cage fronts to be 40–45cm (16–18in) wide and 35cm (14in) high with a similar depth, although depth is less important and is often governed by the width of the thin plywood purchased to make the back and sides. Soft wood strips about 5cm x 1.75cm (2in x ⅝in) wide are used to form a lip at the front of the cage on which to fasten the cage front. They also keep the floor coverings inside the cages as much as possible and provide a means of hanging the feeder and drinker if you use outside fitting utensils.

The inside of the cage should be painted either white (to reflect the light) or a light blue or green. Some fanciers prefer gloss which can be wiped down but I prefer to paint the cage annually or every other year with a good vinyl emulsion.

Cage fronts

I have tried different types, including plastic, which do have advantages, but by far the best, in my opinion, is the solid punch bar front. Although more expensive, they last a lifetime. I spray mine each spring with a black paint available at most DIY stores in aerosol form. By stacking five or six cage fronts on newspaper on top of each other, each one edged to the other, a good finish can be obtained with little waste. When the fronts are fitted to the newly white painted cage it gives the perfect finish.

Floor coverings

Most fanciers use sawdust or soft wood shavings for floor covering. Some fanciers even purchase sterilised sawdust but I have never seen the need for such precautions. I prefer shavings, as sawdust blows about and gets into the water and seed hoppers.

Before putting the shavings into the cage put several sheets of newspaper down. This stops any droppings fouling and staining the floor of the cage where the shavings have moved and makes cleaning out much easier.

Another excellent floor covering material is cat litter. This must be the type that does not dissolve in water. I use Sophisticat, but only for young Fifes from 4–12 weeks old (see chapter 7) and for rearing hens.

Perches

The original fanciers used 1.75cm (⅝in) round dowel but today most fanciers use wooden twist-on perches. Recently I have changed to plastic twist-on perches produced by Superior Birdroom Products, which I find far more hygienic and efficient. Place them as low down in the cage as possible to allow maximum flying space.

Other essential accessories:
(1) Johnson's Anti-Mite (2) Vanodine V-18 500ml
(3) Vanodine V-18 250ml (4) show cage paint (5) 6in wire sieve (6) 8in wire sieve (7) large tube brush (8) small tube brush (9) ³/8in twist perches (10) Yorkshire show cage perches (11) Border show cage perches (12) Fife show cage perches (13) Gloster show cage perches (14) Norwich show cage perches.
Courtesy of Superior Birdroom Products

Feeders and drinkers

These come in a variety of types. I prefer the tubular drinkers as they can be positioned well off the floor, are easily cleaned and the birds will not bathe all the water away in the first hour. Larger tubular drinkers are useful during holidays or when you are housing several birds in a flight cage.

Feeders that fit on to the outside of the cage can be wasteful as the birds invariably flick seed on to the floor. These days I prefer a small, round earthenware dish placed at the back of the cage, away from the perches to prevent fouling.

Electrical equipment

Unlike my grandfather, who had an electric light bulb and open windows, today's breeder uses modern appliances in the birdroom, including:

- ionisers/air filters
- extractor fan
- thermostatically controlled tubular heaters
- dimming lighting systems

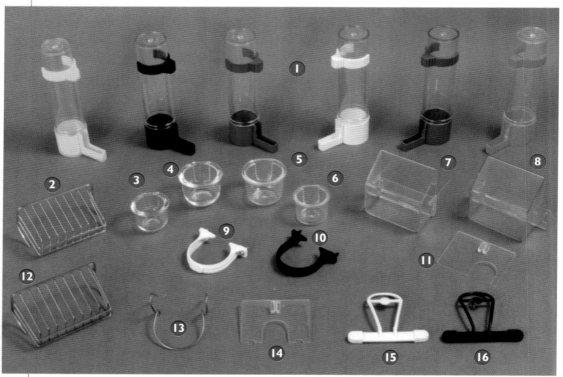

Cage front feeders and drinkers: (1) tubular drinker/feeders 16.5cm (6½in) long 3.8cm (1½in) dia (2) chrome deluxe salad rack (3) glass Fife/Border show cage drinker (4) glass top hat drinker (5) plastic top hat drinker (6) plastic Fife/Border show cage drinker (7) flush-fit seed hopper (wire fitting) (8) flush–fit seed hopper (screw fitting) (9) white plastic top hat bracket (10) black plastic top hat bracket (11) plastic hopper shield (12) breeders' salad rack (13) top hat wire (14) plastic top hat shield (15) plastic cuttlefish holder (white) (16) plastic cuttlefish holder (black).
Courtesy of Superior Birdroom Products

- electric water boilers
- food processors
- industrial vacuums

Ionisers and air filters
It is essential that as much dust as possible is kept out of the birdroom for the comfort of both the birds and the birdkeeper. Ionisers and air filters are available for this purpose.

Ionisers are very useful in this respect and statistics have shown that they improve the breeding success of certain animals and birds. However, they tend to make the birdroom surfaces very dusty. Preferable in my opinion, although more expensive, are the air filters now available. I use the Mountain Breeze air filter which is very inexpensive and easy to maintain.

Tubular heaters
Tubular heaters can now be bought at reasonable prices and, when used with a thermostat, maintain the winter temperature at a sensible level. My bottom row of cages are raised 30cm off the floor to enable tubular heaters to be fitted around the bottom of the birdroom wall.

Having overwintered softbills such as Redstarts and Whinchats at 7°C (45°F) I have found Fifes to be perfectly comfortable at this temperature, which is not uncomfortable for the birdkeeper.

Warning: Do not overwinter Fifes at normal room temperature; otherwise their cycle may be disturbed and they may go into a false moult. Be particularly careful if using paraffin or calor gas heaters in the birdroom.

Lighting systems
Most fanciers today have a lighting system that can be set to come on in the morning and go off in the evening, supported by a dimming system. The latter ensures that the birds are not startled by the light coming on suddenly before dawn in winter and going off suddenly in the evening.

The amount of light on a bird's eye triggers the breeding instinct, and it is wise not to extend the natural hours of daylight more than necessary. For people who work shifts, however, these lights are a very useful aid to winter feeding. If these lights are too expensive then a 25W red bulb in addition to normal lighting can be used to awaken the birds and also encourage them to roost in the evening. Switch off the main light and, after 10 minutes or so, the birds have roosted and the 25W bulb can be turned off. I used this system effectively for many years before the modern equipment came on the market.

Extractor fans
Extractor fans on outside walls are very beneficial in summer to supplement the air filters and ionisers by expelling the old air and drawing in new air through the windows. Xpelair do a good range. When the extractor fan is not in use the flaps drop down, thus preventing small rodents from using the duct as an entry into the birdroom. Prior to the installation of an extractor fan I used an ordinary small household fan.

Industrial vacuums
These are very useful for removing all traces of shavings from around the cage when you clean it out.

Weekly Maintenance

Most fanciers like to clean out the cages weekly and I am no exception, mainly as I work during the week. The weekly routine does not apply to hens incubating eggs, who should be disturbed as little as possible, or to newly weaned youngsters, who are cleaned out every day (see Chapter 7). A weekly clean keeps the birdroom sweet and the birds' feet clean and, most importantly, stops the birds from eating any stale softfood or greenfood.

This is also a good time to offer the Fifes a bath. After a week almost all birds will take readily to a bath. Any that do not should be watched as this is often an early sign that a Fife is off colour.

Good all-wire bathers are available and these can accommodate several birds at once when hung on a flight cage. Do not over-fill the bath — 1 to 2cm (⅜ to ¾in) deep is ample — and cold water straight from the tap is fine. Additives to the water are totally unnecessary.

Once the birds have bathed it is a simple task to remove the wood shavings along with the newspaper covering the cage floor. I used to use a builder's float to go round the cage and lift any surplus shavings but these days I use a small industrial vacuum to clean out all the cages once they are empty.

For those who suffer with breathing problems or develop an allergy to the dust, very good masks are available. At the end of the breeding season and at certain other times of the year I use them. They are reasonably priced and can be obtained from any good DIY stores.

Before I place new newspaper on the floor I spray the cage with Johnson's Anti-Mite Spray to stop any type of mite from becoming established in the birdroom. After that, new shavings, a clean seed hopper, drinker and perches can be added.

Nowdays I clean all feeding and drinking utensils and plastic perches in a small dishwasher, which saves a great deal of time and guarantees a good clean.

Noise in the Birdroom

My grandfather insisted on total silence in his birdroom during the breeding season, and many modern bird books give similar advice. However, I ignore that within reason and the birds do not seem to mind. The dishwasher makes some noise and I also play a radio most of the time I am in the birdroom (particularly *Classic FM* on Saturday morning when I am doing most of my jobs!).

Wild birds nest in the noisiest of places sometimes and the Fifes have become used to a daily routine and do not require any molly coddling.

The Golden Rules of Bird Husbandry...

... good quality feeding, cleanliness and good ventilation.

Chapter
Three Feeding

Like most seed-eating birds the Fife canary has very basic diet requirements:
* a good quality seed mixture
* clean water
* regular greenfood and vegetable matter
* regular softfood
* wild foods
* additives such as grit, cuttle and charcoal

Seed Mixture

There are many good quality canary seed mixtures on the market today. Although some fanciers prefer to mix their own I find Haith's Super or Deluxe canary mixture an ideal basic diet. Most fanciers when mixing their own use plain canary, rape seed and a little niger seed, and many add pinhead oatmeal. At certain times of year this will vary and sometimes certain Fifes are best placed on a diet of plain canary seed. This is covered later on in the book. Top quality seed mixes have all the vitamins, minerals and enzymes necessary to maintain a Fife in top condition.

For a long time I used to mix my own seeds and it was interesting to see which were preferred at which times of the year.

Once, during the 1970s, I experimented by placing separate seeds in separate dishes around the aviary, in which was housed a mixed collection of British finches and canaries. I was very surprised at the high amount of maw seed eaten. The time of year was probably significant.

In another experiment I found that, in very cold weather, my Bullfinches chose

Deluxe Canary Mixture. Courtesy of John E Haith, Cleethorpes. Photo: Geoffrey Pass

linseed seeds in preference to hemp seed in an aviary mixture. Similarly, I would hang up peanut holders in the aviaries in later September. These would be ignored by such birds as Siskins and Mealy Redpolls until some trigger in the environment would see almost frenetic feeding activity on the nuts.

To understand the feeding habits of birds it is useful to understand that all foods are broken down into protein, carbohydrates, fats and water.

Young birds need a high level of protein in their diet.

Some seeds have a very high fat content and are searched out in winter by most birds. The problems begin when birds seek out the fatty seeds without using up the energy that wild birds expend in searching out these foods, particularly in winter.

Detailed analyses are available for all seeds but the fancier only needs to know which have a very high fat content. These include rape, maw, linseed, hemp and niger. All these are available in small quantities in good quality mixtures but, when housed with other birds, one bird can feed entirely on such seeds; you should watch out for this.

Siskins for example can be lazy and put on fat and for that reason I used to feed them on the leftovers from other aviaries. If a bird in a mixed group is putting on weight, then a diet of plain canary and greenfood will slim it down. Canary seed has about 5% fat content whereas maw and rape have about 40%.

The plain canary seed mix is an ideal base and some birds such as Yellowhammers will live entirely on this seed in captivity. It has a breakdown of 50% carbohydrate and 13% protein which, along with the low fat content, makes it a first class base seed.

Conditioning Seed. Courtesy of John E Haith, Cleethorpes. Photo: Geoffrey Pass

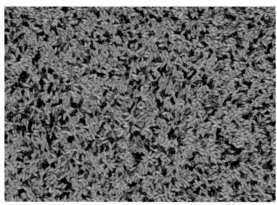

Kraker Tonic. Courtesy of John E Haith, Cleethorpes. Photo: Geoffrey Pass

Foreign Finch Seed. Courtesy of John E Haith, Cleethorpes. Photo: Geoffrey Pass.

Condition seed

In addition to the basic canary mixture of plain canary, rape, niger, hemp and linseed there are other good conditioning seeds to be used prior to the breeding season such as maw, lettuce, gold of pleasure, teazle, and perilla. All have beneficial qualities but the easiest method of supplying these invaluable seeds is by purchasing such a mixture.

Over the years I have developed what I consider to be the perfect mixture for conditioning birds, sick birds, weaning youngsters and so on, and that is:

4kg (9lb)	Conditioning Seed
2kg (4½lb)	Kraker Tonic
2kg (4½lb)	Foreign Finch Seed
0.5kg (1lb)	Perilla

All are available from John E Haith who, as long as I can remember, has advertised weekly on the back page of *Cage & Aviary Birds*.

Water

Do not use additives in the water during hot weather as they will ferment very quickly and could make the birds ill.

At one time I used to add such supplements as Glucodin or Abidec to the drinking water but these days I offer only clean water, preferring to supply all the birds' dietary requirements through natural foods.

It is true that birds like sweetened water. If you hang five jam jar drinking fountains around the garden with only one containing Glucodin you will see that Great Tits in particular will soon identify that one and use it solely!

Greenfoods and Vegetable Matter

Greenfoods are essential to maintain any bird in tip-top condition. Canaries, just like humans, need fruit and vegetables to provide additional vitamins, minerals and roughage.

People who keep one cock canary as a pet in a cage can offer whatever the family are having, such as an outer sprout leaf or a small piece of apple. However, the serious breeder of Fifes should have a proper regime of feeding different greenfoods daily, particularly to young birds, until after the moult. Specific greenfoods to be offered during the breeding and moulting seasons are covered in chapters 6 and 7. All greenfoods should be of the best quality and washed thoroughly before being given to the birds.

With all greenfood, particularly during the moult, the secret is a small amount every day. Do not allow stale greenfoods to remain on the cage or flight cage floor.

The most popular and valuable greenfoods for the Fife are listed below, although I have tried other fruits such as half oranges.

Broccoli

Without doubt broccoli is one of the finest greenfoods available. It can be grown quite easily from seed but these days it is available all year in supermarkets.

In the summer I give this food daily to hens with youngsters in the nest. It can be given as florets and also by cutting the stalk lengthways into quarters, dipping in the condition seed mixture and placing on the cage floor.

Curly kale

Again, this is grown easily from seed but is often available even in supermarkets, particularly in winter when I provide it at least once a week. Fifes prefer this to Savoy cabbage as it has a sweeter taste, but the cheaper greenfoods can also be offered. I see little value in feeding modern grown lettuce as it is mostly water. However, lettuce home-grown in good soil will have a higher nutritional value and can be fed occasionally, although it is not as beneficial as the curly kale.

Sprouts
I prefer to limit these to the best outer leaves and only give one leaf per bird to ensure it is eaten quickly. Avoid yellow outer leaves and soft sprouts that are clearly past their best.

Spinach
Another popular greenfood, this can be purchased in supermarkets but is very easy to grow. Perpetual spinach does not turn to seed as quickly and can be grown over winter to provide soft leaves in the spring for rearing. The seeding heads also are enjoyed by the young birds later in the summer.

Watercress
This is rich in iron and is very easy to grow if you have a garden pond. Landcress is similar and can be grown in ordinary soil.

Rape
Black rape is very easy to grow and provides nutritious leaves as well as yellow flowering heads in the spring when other greenfoods might be in short supply. Roy Fox, my fellow enthusiast, uses a grow bag. A small handful of black rape gives fresh greenfood quickly and

Black rape (cress) growing in a bag on a garden seat.

easily. It is the same as the cress grown for human consumption and can be fed at any stage of growth from 4cm (1½in) high to cabbage plant size. Keep the bag off the ground to prevent contamination by cats.

Carrot
Like many continental breeders I use liquidised grated carrot and kiwi fruit to moisten my rearing food (see chapter 6). Carrot can be cut into long slices in the winter to provide an alternative source of vitamins. To encourage Fifes to try new food such as carrot, dip the slices into the condition mixture.

Apple
Contains natural sugars and is also mixed into my softfoods. Most other times it can be quartered, dipped in condition seed and placed on the floor of the flight cages where it is quickly devoured. An excellent weaning food.

Cucumber
Although I have never tried it myself, several breeders I know place cubes of cucumber on the cage floor, especially in summer. The nutritional value is doubtful.

Chicory
Another popular greenfood particularly during the moult, although it is one I do not use.

Wildfoods

Chickweed
Without doubt the favourite wildfood is chickweed. Large amounts are collected easily in the spring and early summer and it is the ideal conditioner and rearing food for all finch-type birds.

Chickweed tends to appear on newly-turned soil such as motorway verges but after a

Chickweed for conditioning Fifes in spring growing behind the author's birdroom.

year it cannot compete with the grasses and docks and it disappears. It is best located in farmers' fields which are turned over each year. I used to collect large amounts from cabbage, cauliflower and rhubarb fields but these days I no longer have such a supply. Be careful to avoid fields that have been recently sprayed. I grow my own small patch which I use sparingly in the late winter to bring my Fifes gradually into breeding condition.

Dandelion
This is the other favourite wildfood of the bird fancier. Leaves and diced roots can be given in the spring and the seeding heads when the flower is turning white, prior to blowing. There is

no better conditioner for birds that are slow to come into condition in late April or early May. Dandelion coffee made out of the root is also available from health food shops and is a useful winter supplement if given occasionally.

Most wild plants that produce a seed can be given once the seeds ripen: sow thistle, shepherd's purse, meadowsweet, seeding dock (before the seeds go hard and brown), plantain and coltsfoot, which is available as early as February. Groundsel can also be given but avoid the plants with mould on their leaves and only give the seeding head.

If wildfood is in short supply, soaked millet sprays provide a source of soft seed as well as keeping the birds active.

Softfoods

Softfoods and soft seeds are particularly important when young are being reared. This is dealt with in chapter 6.

Food Supplements

Much is made these days of food supplements for cage and aviary birds. I prefer not to use them, as a good wholesome diet of quality seed mixtures, fresh greenfoods and fruit in addition to a rearing softfood is adequate for any small bird such as the Fife. Some additives are given sparingly to assist the moult (see chapter 7) and to sick birds (see chapter 13).

There is a danger of overdoing the supplements, so I prefer to avoid them. However, vitamin supplements and probiotics do have a place if a complete diet is not available and many fanciers now use a probiotic to keep the gut clean.

There are natural supplements to a bird's diet that have been used for many years. These are:

- **cuttlefish bone** which provides extra calcium, particularly for hens in the breeding season, although liquid calcium is now available as an alternative.
- **grit** although there has been much debate over the years as to its benefit. I prefer oystershell grit to mineralised grit. It is thrown on to the flight cage floor after cleaning, particularly in winter…
- …along with a handful of granulated **charcoal**.

As all three additives are relished by the birds when a new supply is offered I can only assume the Fifes derive great benefit from them.

Natural additives like seaweed powder and syrup of buckthorn are used sparingly on the odd occasion, particularly for young birds prior to the end of their first moult.

The basic weekly diet however must always be a good quality seed mixture, greenfoods, wild seeds where possible and a good quality softfood. In my opinion, greenfoods are the secret to maintaining Fifes in perfect condition.

Chapter

Four Purchase of Stock and Winter Management

Purchasing Stock

The time to purchase Fife canaries is from late October until the end of the year. By this time, the established fancier has sorted out the youngsters he or she wishes to retain and has surplus young Fifes and one-year-old birds to sell. No one sells good birds in March or April as, since they have been kept for almost a year, there is little point in disposing of them just as they are about to breed.

Do not purchase a hen that is more than a year old because the breeding life of a Fife canary hen is short. I offer only young birds from the present or last breeding season, although a top-class 2-year-old cock bird can be a very useful investment.

Fifes are often offered for sale as *flighted* or *unflighted* birds. The terms refer to the tail and flight wing feathers, which are not dropped during the first moult. Birds who have never come into moult are referred to as *unflighted*. The following year, these feathers are moulted, and the one-year-old birds are then referred to as *flighted*.

As with all breeds of canary, it is important to start off correctly by purchasing good stock and providing the birds with an ideal environment. Start by looking at the winning birds at major shows, including the National Exhibition of Cage and Aviary Birds. Then select several breeders who appear to have a good stud of birds in different colours – in other words, people who have many good birds. Do not go for the 'one-bird' man – one bird that has won shows but is not part of a good team. Top exhibitors should be able to sell you good birds from their winning lines at reasonable prices. It may be necessary to wait until the following autumn for your birds, but this is far better than purchasing inferior ones, which will lead to disappointment at a future date.

Distinguishing old and young birds

One good way of distinguishing an old bird from a young one is by examining the legs. Those of young birds are quite free from scales and the skin looks soft and smooth. However, individual scales can be seen forming on the legs of the more mature birds. It is also usual to find that the young birds' feet appear cleaner than those of the older ones.

Sexing

A question which is often asked is, "How do you tell a cock from a hen?" Although there is no certain method going by appearance alone, generally a cock has a bolder carriage than a hen: his position is more erect, his appearance bolder and he will be livelier in his actions. As a rule, a cock's head is larger and his plumage has more depth of colour.

Another way to find out the sex of healthy birds, especially during the spring, is by handling them and examining their vents by blowing away the feathers beneath the tail. The vent of the cock bird protrudes, while that of the hen does not.

Topography of the Canary

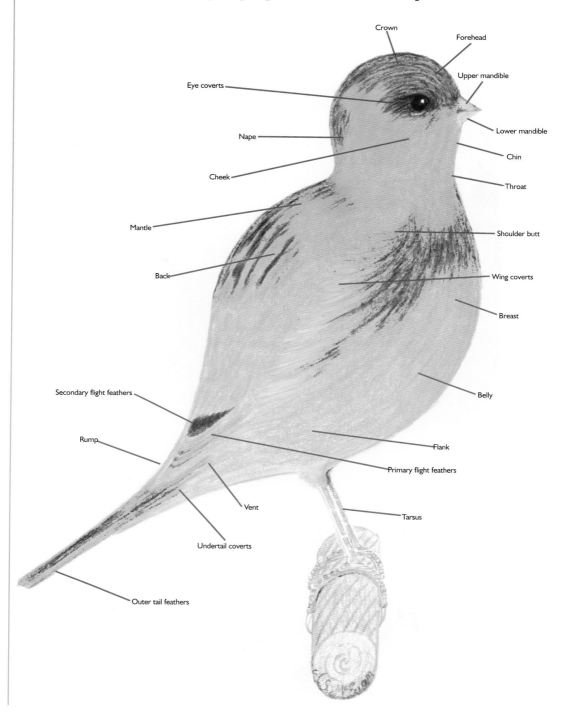

The notes of the cock bird are deeper in tone, more mellow and stronger than those of the hen. When he is in full song, a cock can very easily be distinguished from a hen. This is either at 6–8 weeks or during the spring. Some hens do sing a little, but produce nothing like a cock's full throat warble.

Obtaining the best

You cannot purchase a fancier's best Fifes as he needs them to keep his stud at a high standard. At the National Exhibition as long ago as 1988 I was offered £200 for a self green buff hen Fife – which I refused. You certainly cannot purchase birds that have won shows or done well at the National Exhibition.

However, you can buy siblings and cousins of such birds. My National winner of 1987 was a heavily variegated buff cock, and his brother, a self green buff cock, went to my friend Tony Garvey of Darlington who, for many years, had had one of the top Fife studs in the country. Tony claims he can trace his best Fifes back to that one cock.

The best way to start a small stud is to purchase several pairs and a couple of spare hens. That way, if a hen dies, there won't be a cock without a mate; a cock can be run with more than one hen.

Always purchase the best birds you can afford and start with pairs, which are far easier to manage in the breeding season.

Once purchased, ideally cocks should be caged separately, but this increases the workload, so they can be housed together until they start to come into breeding condition in early March, or even earlier in southern England.

Hens should be provided with the most spacious flight cages available and perches placed at each end of the flight. This will ensure that they have to fly the full length of their quarters, keeping them fit and slim.

Winter Management

Feeding

Feeding is relatively straightforward after the moult and through the winter months. Both cocks and hens should be fed on a canary Deluxe or Super mixture with a little conditioning seed daily.

Birds seem to know what seeds are required at different times of the year, and they will select the oily seeds if the weather is cold.

Fifes benefit from softfood being provided all year round. I try to give the hens softfood once a week, but some fanciers like to give all the birds bread and milk once a week. This aids digestion and helps the older birds, who are more likely to suffer from constipation in cold weather, but greenfood is ideal for avoiding this condition. Feed this just prior to cleaning out the flight cages.

Grit and charcoal (scattered on the cage floor) are also essential at this time.

Fifes should be offered greenfood during the winter months daily. In fact, any fruit or vegetable (cooked or uncooked) that might otherwise end up in the kitchen pedal bin will be inspected by the birds and nibbled at.

All this variety of food helps to keep the birds in good condition during the winter months prior to the breeding season and keeps them active.

To ensure a successful breeding season we should assist the Fife's development gradually over winter to make sure our birds are in good condition by early spring.

Length of daylight

Nature builds up our native birds very gradually – it very slowly releases new foods, daylight lengthens very gradually and temperatures are slow to climb. There is a danger that many fanciers will start to bring their Fifes too quickly into breeding condition rather than assisting this gradual increase in condition.

Recommended maximum daylight lengthening for Breeding

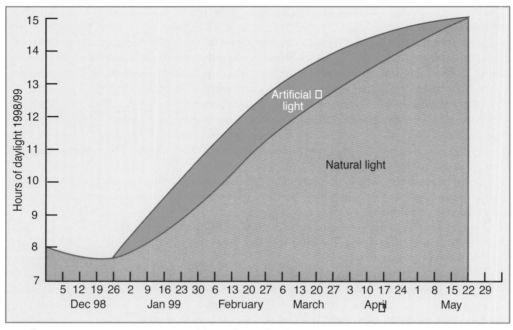

For instance, an inexperienced breeder will often go out and collect large amounts of chickweed in March, when the plant has just started to come through, and give every bird far too much. This sort of treatment will invariably knock the birds back in condition – give them just a little and increase gradually.

Some fanciers like to control the length of daylight their Fifes receive by installing automatic lighting systems that provide artificial light at whatever times required. This is often accompanied by a little additional heat, but the temperature should be no higher than 10°C (50°F). This way the breeding season can be brought forward slightly. Nevertheless, there are dangers if this is not used wisely and the lengthening of the daylight hours is built up too quickly.

It is generally recognised that the best time for canaries to breed is when there are 14 hours of daylight and the temperature is 15°C (60°F). This does not happen until mid-April and even then the temperature is liable to fall below freezing at night. That is one reason why Fifes and other birds often desert their young at this time of year, particularly in a wet spring. Bright, sunny days bring the birds into breeding condition earlier.

Some fanciers start to extend the daylight as early as November if they intend their birds to go down to nest very early. However, Christmas is early enough to start, once the major shows have finished.

Most good calendars have a sunrise and sunset table, so it is easy to extend the daylight by no more than 15 minutes a week from Christmas to the end of March, and then by 10 minutes a week during April and early May, by which time it can correspond with the normal length of daylight and the thermostat can also be switched off, as there should be no more frosts at that time of year.

Conditioners

Daylight is the real natural conditioner that determines when the birds are breeding fit. Many excellent breeding conditioners are available but the most effective ones probably cost nothing. That grand old Yorkshire canary fancier, the late Bill Tennant from Bradford, once told me that the best condition of all was a bath and (as he nudged me) "It costs nowt!"

In winter more than in summer I like all my birds to have a bath mid-week and at weekends as a minimum. Always ensure at this time of year that the birds bathe early in the morning, thus allowing them to dry out by late afternoon when the short winter days cause the birds to roost almost before the afternoon has begun.

My hens overwinter in flight cages that are just over 2m (7ft), and I hang the baths – a wire open type – on the flight cages when I enter my birdroom at 7.00 am. Usually they all bathe immediately. I always check to see that each Fife has had a bath. Most birds learn the routine quickly and are eager to bathe as soon as the bath is offered.

Keep an eye on any bird that refuses to bathe as there is a good chance that it is off colour.

Excess fat

The new year is a good time to examine every bird by hand to see which are carrying excess fat.

The easiest method is to hold the bird on its back and blow back the breast feathers, which will reveal any excess fat just below the skin. Excess fat shows up white rather than the red flesh colour of the normal bird and protrudes slightly above the normal stomach line. Birds carrying excess fat, especially hens, must be given a plainer diet of plain canary seed and greenfood and adequate exercise in the build-up to the breeding programme. Exercise is one of the best conditioners for hen Fifes, coupled with fresh air.

Nails

At the same time, check the nails of the flighted birds, as they will probably need clipping before they can do any damage to the eggs. ***Only remove the tip: ensure that the vein running down the nail is not cut.***

Introducing new foods

Fifes are inquisitive little birds and now, when they are easily managed together in flights, can be the time to experiment with different foods. During the 1970s much of my avicultural activities were centred around the smaller British softbills – Redstarts, Grey Wagtails and Wheatears were particular favourites – and in the winter months I would use Avi-Vite, supplemented with cottage cheese, and cooked potatoes. The smaller thrushes devoured this food. As these birds must be housed away from their own species just prior to the breeding season, I used to place one different type of unrelated softbill in each flight of Fife canaries. Very soon the Fifes learned how good a softbill mixture and cottage cheese was, as well as livefood, surprisingly.

Another useful food in winter for both Fifes and British birds is a chicken carcass, although

I no longer give mine this, due to an improved dietary regime. It keeps the birds occupied as their tiny beaks will search out every scrap of protein. When the Fifes have finished with it, place the remains on the bird table and watch the wild Greenfinches remove any remaining food. Birds benefit from animal protein just as humans do, and feeding them is not just a question of seed and water until a couple of weeks before the breeding season. My friend Gary Pearson, who took Best Novice Fife award at the 1983 National Exhibition of Cage and Aviary Birds, also keeps German Shorthaired Pointers. After cooking meat for his dogs, he places small pieces in his flight cages and these are always picked clean by his hen Fifes.

If you have not already done so, at this time of year the hens should have been introduced to the rearing food on which they will rear their young in the spring. This will get them used to it and will also help in the conditioning process. I used to mix my own softfood which does not go off and is also eaten by British finches and other birds. In a large plastic bin I place 6.3kg (14lb) Haith's Nectablend and add 1.6kg (3½lb) high quality peanuts. Mix these together and then add one packet of Farlene, one packet of Bemax and half a packet of Glucodin. After mixing, add 900g (2lb) pinhead oatmeal, 900g (2lb) minced seed for roughage and 220g (½lb) maw seed. After mixing I add one bottle of corn oil and thoroughly mix the entire contents by hand. This food will not go off, is sweet to the bird's taste and requires no further moisture before being fed to the birds. Many Fife fanciers, and even some homing pigeon fanciers, write to me for this mixture.

From now on hens should be given extra calcium to help them build up their reserves for egg laying. A little cuttlefish bone or liquid calcium should be offered and this will also keep them occupied but hens' eggshells can be baked in the oven and then ground up before you feed them to the hens.

Also at this time of year the fields will be yielding early seeding chickweed and this is probably the finest conditioner available, along with dandelion leaves. These can now be supplemented with a little condition seed mixture at least twice a week as the breeding season approaches.

The birds will show signs of coming into breeding condition in early March or even sooner in sheltered parts of Wales or southern England. Now is the time to place the cocks in single cages where they will be required to breed.

At this point it is a wise precaution to dust every bird with insect powder and spray them with an insecticide spray safe for birds such as Johnson's Anti-Mite. Repeat the process 2 weeks later, preferably in the early morning.

Finally, hang a Vapona block in the birdroom to deter mites. This should be left in the birdroom for the next few weeks but removed a couple of days before the first chicks hatch.

Chapter
Five   Producing a Quality Stud

Once you have purchased some good Fifes from a leading fancier, they should be overwintered with the sexes kept separately so that a pair doesn't form a bond you have not planned.

These Fifes should have been paired up by the exhibitor from whom you bought them in yellow by buff pairings and hopefully some of these pairings – not all – will produce youngsters of quality that equals, or even exceeds, that of their parents.

Buying quality birds related to show winners will always give a fancier an ideal start by raising his own stud to somewhere near championship level in 2-3 years if certain rules are applied.

I recall a novice fancier, Pam Wade from East Anglia, purchasing six pairs of Fifes from me in 1988. It was her first purchase. Her husband kept Yorkshire canaries and she wanted to share his hobby but with a different variety of canary.

In 1989 she produced five youngsters from one of the pairs, who won at many Fife shows. One became Best Novice Fife and Second Best Fife at the National Exhibition of Cage and Aviary Birds in December of that year – her first year in the hobby.

This proves that it is not always easy to assess which Fifes will produce the best youngsters. Had I known that that particular mating would produce such birds, I would have kept them!

If four or five pairs are purchased from the same quality stud there is a fair chance that they are all at least partly related, and some quality

Heavily Variegated Yellow Hen after winning the National Exhibition. This Fife's father has formed the stud for many leading Fife breeders. Photo: Dennis Avon

youngsters will be bred in the first year. If, as in Pam Wade's case, one pair produces winners then that pair and the five youngsters – even if one is not quite so good – should form the basis of your own family line. The cock bird should be paired to his best daughter if one is a yellow and the other a buff feathered bird, and the mother to her best son. The remaining youngsters can be paired to the best of the youngsters from the other pairs, or even brother to sister. This is referred to as *inbreeding,* as distinct from *line breeding,* and needs to be managed very carefully.

Yellow to Buff Pairings

All canaries have two types of feather. One is called *yellow* (which is confusing as half the green and white birds are yellows) or *jonque* and the other is *buff* or *mealy.*

The colouring of a buff feathered bird can be likened to that of a roof whose tiles have been painted white on the edges. The white edge would be quite prominent when the roof was completely tiled. Only the tip of the buff feather is white, but it gives the bird the overall appearance of being dipped in flour with the excess shaken off.

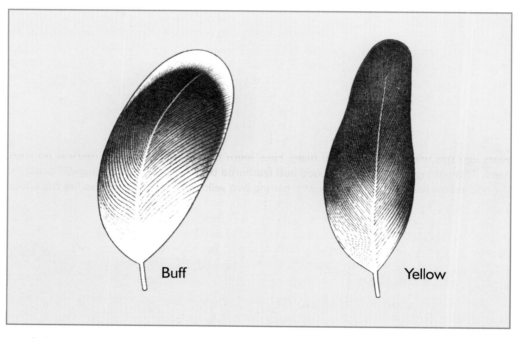

Buff   Yellow

It has long been recognised that to produce a perfect feather quality in canaries it is normal to pair a yellow feathered bird with a buff feathered bird. It does not matter which sex is the yellow and which the buff.

As well as having the white edge, the buff feather has broader webbing than the yellow. The yellow feather is longer and narrower, with the colour extending right through to the tip of the feather.

Although some yellow feathered hens show a little buff, particularly at the base of the neck on the back, cocks never show this buffing. This is a good way of spotting yellow hens exhibited as cocks at Fife shows.

All Fifes – greens, cinnamons and even whites – are either yellow or buff in feather type. It is a myth that all whites are buff feathered.

The type of feathering affects the overall shape of the bird. The buff cocks appear much larger than the yellow hen. The feather bulk creates a false impression. Most buffs appear to lack a clean, distinct neck because of the broader feathering, whereas yellow feathered birds appear thinner. Actually, the body size is virtually the same. Many years ago some American scientists carried out experiments on Woodpigeons which revealed that, when plucked, the largest of the buff cock birds was little larger than the smallest of the yellow birds. It is largely the feather that creates the apparent size difference.

Many articles about canaries also refer to 'hard' and 'soft' feathering. This applies mainly to the heavily feathered variety of canary. It is rather like the difference between fine and coarse hair in humans – soft feathers are fluffy and look as if they have just been washed while hard feathers stick close to the body. However, most Fifes have been bred from yellow to buff pairings and, as a result, their feather quality is far superior to some other popular varieties in which some feather quality has been lost over the years.

The top Fife canaries have a feather somewhere between hard and soft and the top studs in the United Kingdom have superb feather quality. The debates on canary feathering need not worry the novice breeder, but softer feathered Fifes do tend to take longer to dry after a bath.

In some breeds *double buffing* (the pairing of two buff birds) is advocated. This has happened with some of the larger breeds, but also with the Gloster canary, and even the large exhibition Greenfinches on the show bench today. This procedure increased the size of the breed, mainly through broadening the feather. As the Fife is a diminutive breed, this process is of no benefit to the Fife breeder or exhibitor, which is probably why the feather texture of Fifes today is far superior to that of most other breeds.

Some Fife exhibitors recommend pairing a yellow to a yellow to reduce the size. Some years ago this was practised when many Fifes were too large. These days there is no such need. This pairing will produce the odd buff feathered bird just as double buffing will produce the odd yellow feathered bird. However, pairing two yellow feathered birds also has the effect of narrowing the shoulders and producing poor (less than round-shaped) heads, particularly in the cinnamon and white varieties. Until you are an experienced breeder, always pair yellow to buff or buff to yellow unless there is no alternative, in which case double buffing or double yellowing could be tried for one year only. It must be remembered that birds bred from double buffing are unlikely to be suitable for the show bench because of their size, but they could be used as foster parents.

Inbreeding, Line Breeding and Outcrossing

Much has been written over the years about inbreeding and line breeding and the merits of adopting such systems. There are also merits in outcrossing but all the top breeders of all varieties of canaries are there because of a system of line breeding.

Definitions vary slightly, but in general:

- *inbreeding* is the system of breeding from the very closest of matings: brother to sister, mother to son, father to daughter.
- *line breeding* refers to pairings between individuals within one line of descent: half-brother to half-sister, cousin to cousin.
- *outcrossing* is the system of pairing unrelated birds. If good Fifes are purchased this way then a percentage of youngsters produced will be of good quality but to continue this process will not improve the overall quality of the stud.

The Fife fancier who wishes to produce a good strain of birds where most birds have similar characteristics should adopt a line breeding programme. Initially this involves pairing the best youngsters back to their parents. Pairing brother to sister can be used for one year only as I consider this pairing too close to use regularly but, where no cousin or grandparent is available, it will not affect the vigour of the stock. I use brother to sister very occasionally if, for example, I am going to introduce a cinnamon cock bird into my stud, which will have totally different genes. In that case the progeny from the brother/sister pairing will be introduced to new blood.

The purpose of line breeding is to bring the good points (as well as bad) to the surface quickly so that the best of these youngsters have a genetic similarity and we can produce a stud of similar quality.

Perhaps the best illustration of line breeding I read many years ago used the fanciful example of someone theoretically breeding a canary with two heads. The experienced fancier over a period of years would be able to breed a stud of two-headed canaries. In other words, if a cock bird was bred and paired back to his mother, all the young would either have or possess the gene to produce two-headed birds. By keeping the canaries with two heads and inbreeding them such a stud could be formed.

The point being made was that you should apply this system by identifying the best qualities of the Fifes bred when compared to the model (chapter 9). A quality stud will than be produced – if, of course, the ones lacking such qualities are discarded.

Retaining the Best

A stud of Fifes should always revolve around the cock birds because they can control the stud far better than the hens. They can be paired to several hens and tend to breed for longer. Most Fife hens will produce three good breeding seasons whereas a good cock can go on for several more years.

Only retain the very best of your cock birds; even if the cock is used with average hens from the same family (the hens disposed of after one breeding season) the offspring will have half his genes. The hens produced can be used in the breeding programme as the following year the young produced could contain 75% his genes as well as being used in a half-brother/half-sister pairing.

Wherever possible double up on the good points. Birds with good round backs paired to similar typey birds will produce that quality in most of their youngsters. You need to begin with the best Fifes available that have some of the qualities on which you hope to improve.

If producing a quality stud was as simple as line breeding then every breeder in the country would have a top quality stud in every cage. This is not the case.

Weak points must be spotted and the birds discarded. Even then the best cock in your birdroom paired to the best related hen will not produce an entire crop of youngsters of the best quality. For some reason certain birds appear unable to produce all the best features; yet average birds related to them produce a whole crop of youngsters of first class quality.

You may find one cock of good quality, although not the best, consistently produces cock or hen birds of excellent quality. Such birds are invaluable and often form the basis of a top stud.

My National Exhibition winning three parts dark buff cock of 1987 has blood in every green Fife in my stud and this can be traced back over the past 10 years or so.

Colour

As colour is becoming increasingly important in the birdroom, and will continue to do so as the type improves and competition becomes tougher in major shows, it must be taken into consideration when you pair your birds.

When fanciers visit my birdroom in autumn one of the most impressive features to many of them is the depth of colour in my birds. This has taken many years and I have had to follow a few basic rules to achieve it.

Colour is bred into a bird, whether it be a canary, Bullfinch or Blackbird. I have talked to novices at shows who have pale coloured cock birds and they tell me they have fed them on different greenfoods each day throughout the moult, including marigolds and anything else they can find.

If birds have such a poor basic colour then it cannot be improved to a great extent by feeding. Some improvements clearly can be made to the quality of the feather by correct feeding, but only marginally to the colour. My own birds are offered greens all year round, wild plants covered in blackfly – all of which are relished – but the basic colour would come through without these additional items.

The topic of colour is dealt with in detail in chapter 11.

Records

With line breeding it is essential to keep good records. It is no use relying on memory as, hopefully, in time your six clear yellow cocks will be almost identical.

Most fanciers keep a record book and record every bird under the headings 'yellow cocks', 'buff cocks', 'yellow hens' and 'buff hens', giving colour of ring, ring number, strong and weak points, quality of siblings and so on.

The following year the best Fifes are again recorded under these headings but this time the parentage is recorded so that it can be seen that a particular bird is 50% cock A and 50% hen C, for example.

The following year this is repeated so that it can be seen that a particular bird is 75% cock D, and so on. My own records go down to $12\frac{1}{2}$% of a particular bird – in other words, a great-grandfather. With a quality stud it could happen by line breeding that a father of a particular bird is also one of its grandfathers.

My first pairing selection is carried out in September when I have decided which of the year (flighted) birds to keep. These are invariably the birds that have done very well on the show bench the previous year plus the pairings that have produced excellent youngsters, even if they were not from my first team.

The first pairings are made on paper. I know that I am looking for a green yellow hen, for example, to mate to the self green buff cock that was unbeaten at the previous year's Fife shows. I know which pairs are closely enough related to that cock to produce such a hen if he has not produced a self green yellow daughter.

Once I have found those youngsters of top quality to pair back to the flighted birds I select the best of the youngsters. In most seasons I produce a dozen or so self green or three part dark yellow hens and I usually need to retain three or four.

Having selected the one I want for the buff cock and another one I need to pair to my best flighted variegated buff cock, I run the other dozen or so birds into show cages. They are then judged as I would judge at a show without knowing parentage.

I find the selection of a further three green yellow hens from 12 related youngsters difficult as all are very similar in appearance. However, having selected the three to keep, I place the remaining birds in flight cages for disposal at the beginning of November. The buff hens are then judged similarly and a selection is made.

Fanciers have differing opinions on birds, as when I run out a dozen or so green yellow hens for fanciers in November they often prefer the birds in a different order – such is the difficulty of choosing birds of a similar appearance.

Best to best

In December I run all the Fifes for which I have not selected a partner on paper into show cages and choose mates for them, going by appearance but also checking my records afterwards to avoid brother/sister pairings or total mismatches.

Most fanciers, including me, then pair the best yellow cock to the best buff hen, the second best to second best, and so on, until every Fife has a partner. The next stage should be to check for faults; we are attempting to double up on good points, but we do not want to double up on bad ones. For this reason, if once you have paired best to best you find you have a pair where both birds have poor wing carriage or colour or are on the large side, look for alternative mates for each without these faults so that you will produce a good proportion of youngsters without the faults.

If you have several pairs with clearly visible faults it is best to dispose of them and concentrate on a smaller, quality stud. Avoid birds with dropped, crossed or raised wings, broad or dropped tails or poor heads or feather quality.

Many fanciers believe that some qualities are sex linked: that the cock is responsible for size and colour and the hen for type and feather texture. I have no evidence of this, although I have certain Fifes that, for whatever reason, produce quality buffs while others produce quality yellows. Some fanciers say that the best buff cocks will only come from buff cocks, and so on.

Considerable research would have to be undertaken to explore these theories and there may be an element of truth in some of them. For my part, I select my best birds based on parentage and visible qualities. I try also to select birds of similar size.

My best Fifes in the past have often produced good cocks or hens, no matter what the gender. One of the best line of Fifes I ever produced was started by a long buff cock and a tiny yellow hen with very little neck. The youngsters were almost ideal and one youngster from the pair took the Haith's Silver Trophy at the National Exhibition in 1982.

By applying this strategy of retaining the very best, selecting the best youngsters, eliminating faults in pairings and continuous line breeding the new fancier will be able to produce consistent numbers of quality birds after a few breeding seasons. He or she will have the added certainty of producing birds of similar quality in the following breeding season without relying on chance – and there is always an element of chance in adopting an outcrossing strategy.

Judicious Outcrossing

After several years, inbreeding (or even line breeding) tends to weaken a strain despite improving the overall quality of the stud. After many years of inbreeding, canaries often produce more infertile eggs or dead-in-shell or blind chicks. A total outcross will bring in new blood and the resultant youngsters often appear more robust and free from ailments. For this reason, most leading Fife fanciers will bring in an outcross every 3–4 years, not only to introduce a little more vigour but also in some cases to address a particular fault – in the main bringing in an outcross to do a specific job.

Very recently a leading Fife fancier telephoned me to say that many of his birds had developed a very noticeable crease down the chest, although they were good in every other respect.

Views differ on the reason for this crease. All fanciers produce the odd one (usually a yellow bird) with this fault but, like other faults, it can be bred out. One theory for this crease is that it is caused by double yellow pairings or even inbreeding for too long.

This particular fancier wanted two buff cocks with good feather quality and no sign of a crease. As his stud was related to mine it was no problem to provide suitable outcrosses. The birds in question were brought in for a specific purpose.

Often an outcross is available from within one's own stud as most leading fanciers will have two or three different lines within their own birdrooms.

Summary

The golden rules for line breeding Fifes are:

- Start with the best birds available. Several good pairs from one source will save years of time and effort.
- Only retain the best birds. A small stud of good birds is more enjoyable than a large stud of average ones.
- Only breed from fit birds. Unfit birds will bring nothing but problems and will probably fail to reproduce.
- Keep accurate records of parentage and qualities.
- Double up on qualities wherever possible. Never double up on faults.
- Even the best Fifes in the world will produce a proportion of average youngsters. These will possess qualities that might come out in future generations.
- Never double buff Fifes. Only double yellow if there is no alternative or if one of the parents has very soft feathers.
- Bring in an outcross only for a very specific reason, preferably a cock bird.
- Create your own line of Fifes by line breeding and selective outcrossing. Some of the best studs are based on birds from two or more top lines.
- When selecting your pairs or trios you must select birds with the correct type and quality (chapter 9). Try to get a good balance and select birds that can improve the faults in some of your other birds; for example, if a good yellow cock has a poor forehead above the beak then try to remove this fault by running him with a broader feathered buff hen with a good skull.

General note

You must remember that a bird is mostly feather and, if you plucked all the buff cocks and yellow hens in your birdroom, although the buffs would appear much larger in the show cage, the skeletons would be almost identical in size.

Chapter
Six Breeding

By early March the cock Fifes should be in their single cages alongside the empty hens' cages. Hens in the meantime should be kept in their flight cages so that they can continue to exercise and come into higher breeding condition.

The cocks should now be singing lustily and appearing very active. Some cocks will even regurgitate softfood on to the wires or perches.

Pairing up

The traditional and easiest method of pairing up Fife canaries is one cock to one hen. Novices are advised to use this system, certainly in their first year.

Some fanciers use trios (one cock to two hens) or a mixture of pairs and trios. Some leading fanciers will pair an exceptional cock bird to three or more hens.

If you are using a system involving a cock Fife with more than one hen, do not leave him with one hen long enough to form an attachment to her. Failure to apply this rule will inevitably lead to disaster. Invariably he will refuse to mate with any other hen, fight with the others when introduced, infertile eggs will be produced and the whole breeding season will be wasted for the rejected hens.

People often ask me which I prefer: pairs or trios. Due to pressures of work I prefer to use as many pairs as possible as, once they are paired up, there are few problems. I usually set up five trios each year because I have five treble breeder cages and that is a small number to manage. In the past I have run one exceptional cock with three or more hens but it takes time, patience and an element of luck to produce youngsters from all the hens.

Having said that, if a fancier is retired or works shifts and has more time to spend with his birds during the day, a cock can be moved around the birdroom to different hens, particularly later in the summer when all Fifes are in high breeding condition.

Breeding Fit Hens

Unflighted hens come into condition shortly after the cock birds and should be placed in the cages in which they are to breed, alongside the cocks. Usually the one-year-old hens will come into condition a little later and for this reason make a good second hen in a trio pairing.

The problem arises when the cock has two unflighted birds in his trio. One hen will almost certainly reach breeding condition before the other. The cock will show more attention to this hen; she will be responding and he, particularly if he is unflighted, will be keen to mate with her.

If the second hen is clearly well behind the first, it is as well to let the cock mate with the first, but only allow him into the cage to mate – return him to his own cage immediately afterwards. Once this hen has laid a clutch of eggs she will show no further interest in the cock bird for the time being and his attention can now be aimed at the second hen. During the 2 weeks in which the first hen is building a nest and laying a full clutch of eggs, the second hen should have come more into high breeding condition.

The difficulty of establishing a trio arises where there is little difference in breeding condition in the two hens and both are ready to go to nest. In this case, only allow the cock bird sight of the hen for a few minutes at a time. Pull one partition out half a centimetre just for a few minutes each day. Do the same with the other hen but allowing him to see the hen that is behind in condition for a little longer.

If both hens are ready they can be allowed to build with careful rationing of the cock's time. Allow the cock bird into each cage a few minutes at a time. If mating takes place, remove him right away. If the pair fight, one of them (usually the hen) is not ready for breeding and she should be left for a few days before you try again, although during this period the partition should still be pulled back slightly every day to test her reaction.

A hen in good condition will squat and want to mate immediately. My hen that was Best Fife Hen at a recent National Exhibition will respond like this as soon as she sees her usual mate, even though he is now very old and cannot sing a note. An unflighted bird is uncomfortable with a cock bird that cannot sing, but a pair bond is never forgotten in the older birds.

When to Pair – Regional Variations

Living as I do in the north of England, I find that early to mid-April is the time my Fifes are ready for pairing up, and this coincides with the time I place my British finches in outdoor aviaries. In southern England, Wales and indeed in certain areas in the west of Scotland, birds reach breeding condition earlier because of the milder climate, but this will vary from year to year and it is best to leave pairing as long as possible to ensure that fertile eggs are obtained in the first round.

The Mating

If introduction has been gradual, as advocated, the cock bird will pull himself in when in the presence of the hen, pick up a piece of wood shaving and hop around before her with this potential nest material in his beak. If she does not respond by threatening him, the pair will not be far away from mating and a nest pan with a small amount of outer nesting material such as grass or moss can be introduced into the hen's cage.

Many breeders these days introduce the nest pan along with nesting material well before a cock is introduced. Once a hen appears to be building in earnest and pushing the material into place with her legs then she is ready to mate and the cock can be introduced. Mating usually takes place instantaneously.

As has already been mentioned, a hen squatting is an indication that she is ready to mate. A flighted cock will usually mate right away and the pair should then be separated. An unflighted cock may be wary of a hen in this position calling for a mate, and a little patience might be needed before a successful mating takes place.

Nest Pans

Hen Fifes in breeding condition will build a nest wherever they feel they can make a circular cup to hold the eggs. Many years ago I placed a spare pair of Bramblefinches in a very small aviary and they nested on the floor as no nest sites had been provided.

Hen Fifes will nest on the floor initially if they are not happy with their nest pans,

Nest pans and materials: (1) wooden nest pan (2) plastic nest pan (3) clay nest pan (4) cotton nesting material (5) jute nesting material (6) wool nesting material (7) clay nest pan wire bracket (8) square wool nest felt (9) jute nest felt (5in dia) (10) wool nest felt (11) nest pan splash back (12) dummy eggs. Courtesy of Superior Birdroom Products

particularly if wood shavings are placed on the cage floor, offering the chance to make a nice nest. Similarly, newspaper will be pulled up and used.

Most fanciers these days prefer the white plastic nest pan that fits on to the front or the side of the cage. Square wooden ones with a zinc gauze base are also popular and older fanciers still swear by old earthenware pans as these do not sweat.

A felt lining should be sewn or stuck with soft carbolic soap into the pan with the odd sprig of moss dropped in for good measure to encourage the hen to start building there.

The pans I have preferred for many years are the ones that fix on to the cage front. This makes routine maintenance and inspection very easy and the droppings fall clear of the cage walls.

Nest Building

Some hens lay directly into the lining, but this should not be encouraged. Soft nesting material in the form of moss raked from the lawn or purchased from a nurseryman is ideal. Dry soft grass is also useful for the other structure.

When the nest is well under way, softer substances such as jute and cotton-based nest materials can be offered by placing them on the outside of the cage in a wire holder to ensure the hen only receives small pieces at a time.

If you are using trios, do not allow the cock to become involved in nest building. Run him into the cage each morning until the second egg is laid – no further matings are necessary after this.

As the nest develops the hen will know when to call to the cock, particularly when she is on the nest. Try to ensure that the cock is running with the hen on these occasions. Remove each egg as it is laid and replace it with a plastic dummy egg.

If you don't see mating taking place then try again in the evening. If a pair has not commenced nest building after 7 days, remove the pan and do not attempt to pair up the birds for a further few days.

Variegated Yellow Fife hen on a nest pan fixed to the front of the cage.

Egg Binding

Fife hens in good condition rarely become egg bound but occasionally they will do so during the colder spring mornings. It is the contraction of the muscles around the vent that causes the problem but a fit hen should be able to pass the egg at temperatures marginally above freezing point. An egg bound hen is easily spotted as she will be sitting on the cage floor in a huddled ball. Gently remove her and place her in a hospital cage at approximately 32°C (90°F) or move her in her breeding cage to a warm, quiet spot (near a radiator is ideal) in the house. If the egg has not been laid by evening, place the cage in the airing cupboard and hopefully next morning, having passed the egg, she will be hopping about as though nothing has happened.

Do not try to force the egg or apply oil to the vent, as the bird is then more likely to panic, which will have the reverse effect of relaxing the vent muscles.

I have had several thousand Fife eggs laid in my birdroom and I have never lost a young hen through egg binding. I have seen this condition in other birdrooms and I am of the firm view that it is found in over-fat hens that have not had sufficient exercise in the build-up to the breeding season. Such hens have poor muscle tone which hinders the ability to push backwards, and a sudden drop in temperature worsens the problem as this too reduces the muscle activity. This condition has a rapid onset and a rapid demise which can result in death or hopefully a speedy passing of the egg.

Older fanciers like my grandfather used to recommend holding the bird over a steaming kettle, but this will scald the bird and no doubt induce shock. As a final resort, hold the bird over boiling water placed in a bowl and lubricate the vent gently with a water-soluble lubricant, and then immerse the bottom half of the bird in warm water to warm and contract the vent muscles.

Some old bird books recommend feeding extra niger seed to prevent egg-binding. In my opinion, this is false advice, as niger is a very oily seed and can only help put on additional fat.

Hatching

Eggs should be removed and replaced by dummies until the fourth egg is laid and then 'set'

One-day-old chick. Note that the eggs on either side are dark, denoting fertility.

(placed under the hen). Once the eggs have been set they should hatch at 13–14 days of incubation. It is normal to set the eggs on the morning the fourth egg is laid. Continue to feed the cock birds softfood and greenfood through this period, as well as the hens which have not reached breeding condition.

There is no thrill quite like seeing the first eggshell on the cage floor, which tells you that the first major hurdle has been successfully cleared.

On the afternoon of the 13th day of incubation I place a small amount of rearing food in an eggfood drawer and place it in position

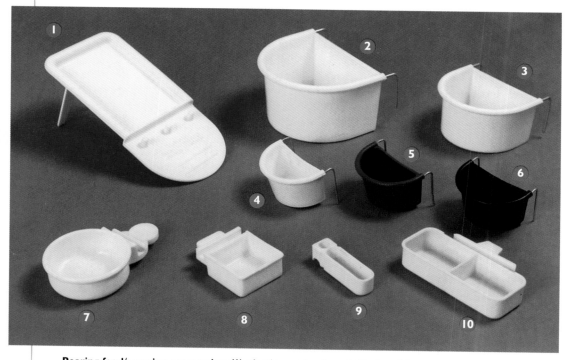

Rearing food/weaning accessories: (1) plastic pecking board (2) giant 2-hook drinker (3) large 2-hook drinker (4) small white 2-hook drinker (5) green 2-hook drinker (6) black 2-hook drinker (7) round egg drawer (8) square egg drawer (9) finger drawer (10) double egg drawer.
Courtesy of Superior Birdroom Products

for the hen that evening or the following morning. Occasionally, eggs will hatch after 12^{1}/$_{2}$ days. This is unusual, but keep an eye on the cage floor just in case. A hen will tend to sit higher in the nest as chicks are hatching or newly hatched and this will be a good guide. Do not rely on eggshells on the cage floor each time as many hens eat the shells as soon as they are hatched.

Some fanciers test the eggs for fertility at approximately 8–9 days and destroy them if they are clear. I prefer to leave the eggs and allow the hen to sit the full 2 weeks. If they are removed too early she may not be inclined to nest again right away. If she is left to sit her full spell then her instinct will tell her something is wrong and she will want to nest again without any encouragement.

Some eggs hatch after up to 16 days, so do not destroy prematurely. I have done this on occasions, only to find an almost fully-formed chick inside.

Rearing Foods

Young Fifes need a diet of softfood, greenfood and a softseed in the form of chickweed or soaked seed.

Each type of rearing food should be given fresh at least daily whether it be chickweed, softfood, greenfood, soaked seed or a mixture of these. Offer softfood at least twice a day and greenfood daily. Increase the supply of rearing foods offered as the youngsters grow.

Once the chicks have hatched, offer soaked seed, chickweed and softfood in very small quantities and leave the hen to get on with the job of rearing. Very little food will be taken for the first few hours, but leave the hen a selection of rearing foods. Some will go for the softfood initially, some for the chickweed or the soaked niger in the mixture.

A Cinnamon Variegated chick and a Fawn and White chick at 14 days old. Both of these are hens: the father was Cinnamon and the mother White. All the daughters carry the colour but the sons do not, so they can be sexed at birth.

One hen I had went straight for the fresh spinach (it was late in the season and chickweed was not available) and fed all four chicks large amounts of this valuable greenfood almost on hatching. All were successfully reared, so do not withhold a particular rearing food for a few days after hatching. Leave the dry seed mixture in the hoppers for the hens.

Five healthy chicks at 16 days old. Note the deeper yellow throats of the two cocks.

Do not neglect the single caged cocks during this period but feed them regularly on small quantities of the rearing, conditioning and greenfood.

Softfoods

Many softfoods are available today, all of very good quality, and it is really a question of personal choice and availability. Haith's Nectarblend, Cede, EMP and Sluis are perhaps the most popular and these can be supplemented with butcher's sausage rusk or pinhead oatmeal added to the softfood before the water, but I find this unnecessary.

Some fanciers prefer to make their own mixture and a high protein one with a peanut base is described in chapter 3.

Nectarblend. Courtesy of John E Haith, Cleethorpes. Photo: Geoffrey Pass

My grandfather, along with most other canary fanciers, always added hard-boiled egg to the softfood. I used to scramble large amounts of egg and place them in small containers in the freezer – that way they can be lifted out daily.

Over the last few years I have tried to avoid rearing foods which are likely to go off in warm weather and I have stopped feeding egg in any form. I prefer to moisten the softfood with liquidised fruit and vegetable. I place carrot and broccoli with a small amount of water in the liquidiser for a minute, and then I add an apple and a kiwi fruit and liquidise for a further minute. This is then added to the softfood. This mixture provides the ideal vitamins and texture but some fruits such as pear are not as effective.

Roy Fox regards cous cous as a valuable softfood; either one measure of cous cous to two measures of cold water left to soak for 20–25 minutes then dried off with any commercial brand (only a small amount) to make a crumbly mix, or it can be given 'straight'.

Greenfood

Fifes enjoy all greenfoods but I prefer spinach and broccoli for rearing purposes. The florets of broccoli and perpetual spinach leaves grown in the garden are relished by the rearing birds.

These are used as an alternative to collecting chickweed although I do grow a small patch of chickweed behind my birdroom as a change of diet.

Soaked seed

Young babies cannot easily digest hard seed so seed should preferably be offered at the soaked and sprouting stage. Black rape seed is ideal for this purpose and Haith's Easisoak is a good mixture for soaking.

The process is relatively simple to carry out. Place sufficient seed in a lady's nylon stocking (half a pair of tights these days!) and soak it for 24 hours in a small bucket of cold water. Rinse this and allow it to hang for a further 24 hours. The excess water will drain off, the seed will start to sprout and the seed's sugar content will be at its highest.

Give them the soaked seed fresh daily in a separate dish. It is a simple matter to have a couple of buckets rotating so that fresh seed is available daily.

Bathing

Baths should still be offered throughout this period, particularly the morning the young hatch. Most hens enjoy a bath at this stage. Some bathe regularly during incubation as the moisture assists hatching but others refuse during this period.

Sweating Hen

As the young progress the hen will continue to swallow their droppings for the first week or so. This is perfectly natural and they pass straight through her. Some fanciers add a little Epsom salts to the drinking water at this period, but I have found this to be unnecessary if a good supply of greenfood has been maintained.

Very occasionally a hen may appear wet on the underside and the youngsters' down appears wet. The bird then has the condition known as 'sweating hen'. This can be avoided in a well run birdroom and views differ on the cause. The most common is diarrhoea in the youngsters. Clean out the nest and offer the hen a little antibiotic in her water.

Soaking seed for rearing babies. Place the soaked seed mixture in a nylon stocking and soak in a bucket of water. Soak for 24 hours , rinse and then hang for 24 hours until it sprouts.

Re-introducing the Cocks

When using pairs it is wise to re-introduce the cock to the hen several days after the young have hatched.

If he is re-introduced too quickly the hen might attack the cock in defence of her young. The first 5 days of rearing are crucial – after this, success is usually assured.

During incubation I leave the partitions half a centimetre out so that contact can be maintained by the pair.

The hen will leave the baby Fifes more frequently when they are 3 days old and at this stage I offer the cock softfood and greenfood when I offer the hen these rearing foods. This way he will feed her at the back of the cage with these foods.

After a couple of days, pull the partition further out so that the cock can enter the hen's cage. He will then instinctively start to play a part in the rearing of the young. The sight of gaping youngsters triggers the instinct to regurgitate food into their mouths. However, re-introducing the cock when chicks are feathered with eyes open will often have the opposite effect.

Second Rounds

The cock will continue to play his part and will take over the bulk of the feeding as the hen prepares to nest again.

A cut down CéDé box keeps youngsters warm after an early nest explosion at 12 days. The flap closed for 30 minutes when the babies are put into it gets them to settle – and parents cannot resist an open mouth!

After about 2 weeks the hen will be showing signs of wanting to go to nest again; she will call to the cock bird and carry nesting material around. The nest pan with the youngsters inside can be placed on the floor and a second pan inserted into the cage. I prefer not to do this as it is likely to cause the youngsters to leave the nest too early – *nest explosion* is the term used among bird fanciers.

If a second pan is not introduced early enough the hen will start to build on the floor or re-line the existing nests. Place the new pan on the opposite side of the cage front at the 2-week stage whether you are using pairs or trios.

If young birds jump out of the nest at 12 or so days old they cannot be returned as they will just jump out again, which can make successful rearing rather slim. Leading Fife fancier Roy Fox has a remedy for nest explosion: he places an empty eggfood box on the cage floor and places the youngsters inside after opening up an entrance through which the parents can feed them.

Provide fresh nesting material and, with trios, when she has started to build a second nest run the cock bird back into the hen's cage. At this stage mating should take place almost immediately. If it doesn't, do not leave the cock with the chicks too long as he might attack the youngsters in the nest.

The first egg should be laid when the first round youngsters are 18–19 days old and the setting of the second clutch should synchronise with the weaning of the first round chicks. Remove these youngsters when they start to pick up food from the floor, which will be at 22–23 days old.

The youngsters can be a nuisance at this stage as they are liable to occupy the new clean nest and prevent the hen from incubating the eggs; therefore try to set the eggs after the young have been weaned by delaying for a few days if necessary.

Now is the time to give the breeding cage a good clean out. Run the hen into a show cage and quickly remove the old floor covering. Spray floor with Johnson's Anti-Mite or similar, place clean newspaper and wood shavings on the floor and change the perches. Place a little granulated charcoal, oystershell grit and cuttlefish bone on the floor, and the hen is ready to commence her second round of incubation in good clean surroundings.

Breeding Season Tips

1   *Do not pair up unfit hens* They will invariably let you down. Some Fifes will lay a clutch of eggs in March–April and then desert. This is a clear sign they were not ready. The eggs will almost certainly be infertile. Condition the hen for a further week and re-introduce the nest pan. Breeding fit hens carry the nesting material at the back of the beak.

2   *Egg binding* Prevention is better than cure. Ignore the old wives' tale that you should give them extra niger prior to breeding season. Give them less fatty seeds and more cuttle (or calcium) prior to the breeding season.

3   *Single chicks hatching* These tend to be harder to rear than two or three primarily because the chick rolls about. Try to synchronise the bulk of the hatchings even if it means not setting the clutch of the first Fife to lay until a week after her first egg. Rather than have one nest of one youngster and another of five, make them three and three. Put two dark birds with the one clear so that you can identify the fostered youngster. If this cannot be done then crop the down from the moved chicks to identify them even at 14 days when a plastic ring can be placed on its leg. If there are no fosters available leave one egg to assist balance. The one chick could also fall between four or five clear eggs and die.

4   *Dead in shell* Many reasons are put forward for this but I think the idea of eggs becoming chilled is nonsense. My father once put some goose eggs under a broody poultry hen which hatched on time although he waited 2 weeks to set them. I have had ice cold eggs from a hen who had deserted hatch on time under another hen. We need more research.

5   *Deserting the eggs after a few days* The hen does not sit all day so don't be too wary just because she has been off the eggs for half an hour. Test the temperature of the eggs with your lips, which are more sensitive than your fingers. If after a few hours the eggs are stone cold, mark them with a felt-tip pen and transfer them to another hen (or hens). Place dummies in the nest to see if she is going to go back to her nest, in which case the eggs can be returned.

    A sick hen will desert and she should be put on antibiotics and left to recover for at least 2 weeks. It is unlikely she will rear her chicks successfully after an illness.

6   *Clear eggs* If the hen appears fit and produces clear eggs then, if I have synchronised my hatchings, I will give that hen a couple of youngsters from a large clutch. That way she will eat the softfood and chickweed over the next 3 weeks and then lay fertile eggs, as she will be in breeding condition. To put a fresh pan in where the eggs do not hatch may only produce a second round of clear eggs and all that energy and effort has been wasted.

7   *Overdue eggs* Do not be too anxious to remove eggs if they have not hatched after 14 days. Some people find it difficult to know whether a chick is dead in shell or about to hatch. Leave the hen 17–18 days; she will leave them when she knows they will not hatch. Even then, chip off the top at the large end where the air sac is, just in case a live chick is inside.

8   *Youngster falls out of nest* Chicks are often pulled out of the nest accidentally during the first few days of their life. They will appear cold and dead. Place them in your closed hand and the heat may trigger a positive heartbeat which you will feel. The chick can then be placed back under its mother.

9   *Deserting the chicks* If a hen deserts the youngsters for whatever reason then the cock will also probably abandon them. If you are convinced the chicks have not been fed for several hours, crop the down on top of their heads (for easy identification) and move them to another mother. Reshuffle the chicks so that they are about the same size as the

others in the nest. If you take the young from one nest at 3–4 days old and replace them with youngsters 6–7 days old there should be no problem.

Desertions at over 2 weeks old occur very occasionally when the hen is too keen to go to nest again. The odd chick can be dropped into a full nest, hopefully without rejection or desertion of the whole clutch.

10 *Hand rearing* If a youngster not old enough to be weaned but too large to transfer is deserted, it will have to be hand reared. Purchase a 5ml syringe from the chemist and mix a paste of Hagen Tropican hand rearing food. Feed the chick regularly on this until it can be weaned at 21 days.

11 *Squashed chicks* The first 5 days of a chick's life are the most crucial and some hens continue to sit too tightly. These hens appear to be too low down in the nest – a hen with hatching babies will appear high up on the nest so that she does not suffocate them. If you have suspicions, remove the pan for 5 minutes to let the hen feed on the softfood. She may not feed the chicks when she returns to the nest but will hopefully do so shortly after she has eaten the rearing food.

If the chicks die, put a fresh pan on the other side of the cage; the hen will brood the empty nest pan if it is left in the original spot.

Hand rearing a baby Greenfinch – it would be the same for a Fife. The use of a syringe is essential for success.

12 *General movement around the birdroom* I have moved a nest of young and the hen from one cage to another with no effect, such is the strength of the rearing instinct of a breeding fit Fife hen. When Andrew Lindsey from Glasgow stopped keeping Fifes several years ago it was towards the end of the breeding season. Alan Pennington from Carlisle purchased his entire stud and moved some of the chicks in a shoebox. As soon as they were placed in a cage 100 miles away the hen started to feed them!

13 *Clothes pegs as markers* I use white, blue and red clothes pegs in my birdroom to hold the cage front door open, which gives me one free hand while carrying out routine tasks. They also make managing a stud easier. I use red pegs to denote youngsters in the nest, blue pegs on a clutch of eggs which has been set (therefore no additional work is needed for 2 weeks) and white pegs to denote a clutch being laid or an egg to be removed. Thus my cages move from white to blue to red pegs. It is also useful if you are away and someone has to give them softfood – just feed the occupants of the cages with red pegs. Pegs and a diary are used instead of record cards and it works far better on a day-to-day basis.

14 *Breeding season* The breeding season is much more enjoyable if it is delayed and kept shorter. You don't want chicks as well as clear eggs and other related problems from March to September. Don't breed too many youngsters, which then become a bind and spoil the pleasure of breeding. As a golden rule, have youngsters hatch in the three months of May, June and July.

Chapter

Seven Weaning and Moulting

Weaning

At 18–19 days old the young Fifes start to venture out of their nest and explore. Several days later they will leave the nest in earnest. At this time they will start to peck at most things to see what is edible and at 22–24 days old they will start to eat the broccoli or softfood placed in the cage. Now is the time to wean them.

Do not follow the recommendation of old canary books and remove them at 21 days. This is usually far too early and will almost certainly lead to unnecessary deaths.

Place the young Fifes in twos and threes (you might lose one out of a clutch of 5–6) in small cages with newspaper on the cage floor. I prefer to use training cages which are similar to but larger than show cages, but show cages will do. I place kitchen roll on the floor of these as it is more absorbent – for a few days the young Fifes will spend a lot of time on the floor.

Under no circumstances place perches in this cage.

Several years ago at a North of England FFCC club meeting a fellow fancier told me he lost many youngsters once they had been removed from their parents. He dreaded this part of the breeding cycle. Although he offered them bread and milk, softfood and so on, many birds died.

From years of experience I didn't need to ask further questions to know what was causing this tragedy. "You put perches in the weaning cages, don't you?" I said to him, knowing this would be his downfall.

Weaned young in training cages at 22–24 days.

A young bird at this age, whether a wild Greenfinch in the garden with its unmistakable begging call or a baby Fife removed from its parents, will sit on a perch and call, expecting one of the parents to fly in and feed it.

Next Stage

Food

Young birds must be offered a selection of foods (ideally in the same type of receptacle as the parents used) placed on the floor so that they are literally standing in the food. Offer the softfood, greenfood rinsed under the tap and an apple quarter dipped in my recommended condition seed. Within minutes at least one young Fife will be pecking at the seeds on the apple or on the greenfood and sampling the softfood. Very soon they will all follow – and they are weaned.

This process has enabled me to wean 388 young Fifes over the past four breeding seasons and 385 got through the moult successfully. Not included in that figure are a handful of weaklings who clearly were not going to make it. I did not ring them but hadn't the heart to kill a bright-eyed youngster enthusiastically tucking into its food.

On the day after weaning I place a perch in the training cage as low down on the floor as possible. The next day I place a second perch at the other end of the training cage.

Replace the kitchen roll and old food daily and change the perches.

Ringing

On the third day I remove the youngsters, clean their feet and place a numbered, coloured plastic ring on one of their legs. These are called *split rings* as each ring has a split in it, allowing it to be expanded as it is held in the small tool supplied with it for that purpose. The open ring is then placed on the tarsus (leg) of the bird and squeezed together between thumb and forefinger so that it remains in place but moves freely around the leg. A C Hughes, who advertises weekly in *Cage & Aviary Birds*, is one supplier of these rings, which come with easy-to-follow instructions.

Sexing

At this stage, or even earlier, it is usually easy to sex your stud by colour alone. The young cocks, especially the clears and variegates, will appear much brighter in colour, particularly at the throat. This does not indicate buff or yellow feathers as buff cocks will be brighter coloured at this stage than yellow hens.

Baby flight cages (2.1 metres (7ft) long) newly painted.

Green Fifes are easier to sex after they have moulted out as cocks; hens have different lace markings as well as differing slightly in colour and size. That is why novices should not try to exhibit green hens in the cock classes before an experienced judge!

Moving on

I place the ringed youngsters in the small end section of one of my long flight cages, which is only 30cm (12in) wide. Into this end compartment I have placed several layers of newspaper with one perch very low off the floor and the rearing foods on the floor. The youngsters will continue to recognise the food and conserve energy by sitting on the one perch.

When they are 4 weeks old or so I remove the partition separating the 30cm end compartment to allow the youngsters into a 60cm (24in) compartment, usually to make room for the next batch of youngsters. My flight cages can be divided into one approximately 30cm and three approximately 60cm compartments.

The youngsters are still fed on the same food with the newspaper changed every day. To do this I move the youngsters from compartment to compartment. When all three main compartments are occupied with youngsters, the small end section enables me to move the three sets of youngsters down one compartment each and clean out one at a time before moving them back. Carry out this procedure every other day and replace the newspapers and perches. This way excrement and old food will not be picked up by the youngsters.

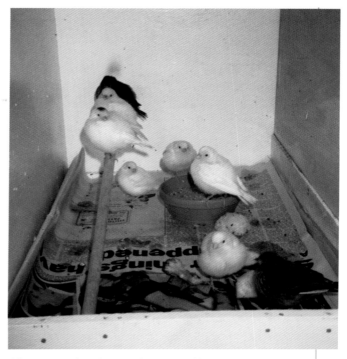

Next stage after the weaning cages. Change newspaper, food and perches daily.

Hard Seed

At the 4-week stage I introduce the youngsters to hard seed. Some old canary books recommend delaying the introduction of hard seed until much later, stating that they will not be able to digest the seed. This is nonsense: young Fifes will eat hard seed as soon as they start to pick up.

The seed mixture I offer them is my conditioning mixture made up of Haith's Kraker Tonic, condition seed, Foreign Finch Tonic and perilla. At this stage I also offer water with no additives in tubular drinkers. The drinkers are cleaned every other day when I clean out the cages.

Enteritis

Some fanciers lose many youngsters through enteritis or 'going light' at the 6–8-week stage. Mainland European canary keepers do not experience this problem to the same extent and in some western European countries it is known as the 'English disease'.

Youngsters die from enteritis very quickly if they pick up and eat stale greenfood or stale softfood, including hard-boiled or scrambled egg. Almost all fatalities of young Fifes before their first moult are due to this one disease.

Enteritis in young Greenfinches has been a talking point as long as I can remember. Different drugs were tried – firstly sulphur-based drugs, then Terramycin – and some fanciers used to lose many of their birds.

In my view it is all down to cleanliness and not allowing the birds access to any mouldy food. Some species are clearly more susceptible than others because of their normal diet in the wild. Bullfinches, for example, eat softfood for most of the year, whether it be buds or autumn fruits. Only for several weeks in the late summer do they sample hard seeds. Consequently, they are far healthier on a soaked seed diet. Chaffinches on the other hand eat the 'chaff' after the harvest (hence their name) and will forage in cowsheds for hard seeds. Because of this inheritance I cannot remember ever losing a Chaffinch once it was weaned, either as a youngster or as an adult; they obviously have an effective immune system.

Suitable floor coverings

I used to suffer my own share of losses up to 15 years ago when I discovered that continental breeders do not use sawdust as a floor covering. All birds eat in small quantities whatever is placed on the floor and I am reasonably convinced that the sawdust caused problems when eaten by young birds. The ideal floor covering, which I introduce at the 5–6-week stage, is cat litter. Some types of cat litter are earth-based and soluble in water and should be avoided. The small, hard, white chippings that do not dissolve in water are what is required. I use Sophisticat as it is readily available in most pet shops.

At first the young Fifes will start pecking at it and appear to consume a fair amount. This has had no detrimental effect and probably acts in the same way as grit in the gizzard.

Once they are past 8 weeks I feel confident cleaning the cage floor out just once a week, after the young birds have had a bath. Go on removing greenfood and softfood daily but, if you provide additional cat litter, the cage cleaning can be reduced to once a week without any detrimental effect. This certainly makes life easier towards the end of summer when (hopefully!) all the flight cages are full.

The moult

All birds need to keep their feathers in excellent condition. This is important not only for insulation but also for flying after prey, whether it be a Grey Wagtail after a fly or a Sparrowhawk after a small bird. That is why birds bathe regularly and appear to bathe more frequently when the weather is cold and the water is just above freezing point. Maintaining the feathers in good condition will ensure more protection in the coldest of weather.

Annual replacement of feathers

All birds replace their feathers annually. Most birds, both young and old, moult out in late summer, when the old feathers are replaced by new.

The condition of a Fife's feathers will influence the judge more than anything else. The rise on the back of the Fife is partly due to the condition and quality of the feather, and the overall texture and sheen separate a quality show bird from an also-ran.

Young Fifes, like all finches, have down on their heads and backs when hatched. As the feathers begin to grow their soft central cavity is fed by blood vessels, which supply pigments as well as food.

Once the feather is complete it hardens, the blood supply stops and it is firmly gripped by the feather follicle in the skin until the following moult. Feathers grow in areas called *feather tracks*. Remove a feather and it is replaced in a few weeks.

The start to the moult is triggered by the reduction in daylight and a hormone change once birds have reared successfully. There is a sequence to the dropping of different feathers. Wing and tail feathers start to drop first and the head feathers are the last to be replaced. The tail and wing feathers are replaced slowly and precisely, as losing too many feathers at once would impede flight and leave the bird vulnerable to predators. Predators such as Sparrowhawks moult one feather at a time from each side of the wing so that their flight is not inhibited. Most birds of prey moult very slowly for most of the year for this reason.

Unflighted birds

Birds in their first summer do not moult their tail and wing flight feathers, which is why they are referred to as unflighted birds. Only in the second summer do they moult their tail and flight feathers.

Fanciers used to view the moult as a sickness. It is no such thing: it is a natural phenomenon, but it does need to be handled differently. Growing feathers, for example, need additional protein to the normal diet. The birds in the wild, even the friendly Robins, become shy during this period, and this behaviour should be respected.

Timing the moults

Try to make the moult as quick, healthy and clean as possible by:

- avoiding stress by allowing the birds to moult out in the same flight cage. A sudden shock could stop the moult temporarily.
- continuing to feed them on rearing foods and greenfood, particularly the colour enhancing ones, until well past the moults.

The first moult should last for 8–10 weeks. Young Fifes bred in April will start their moult at 10–12 weeks old; the ones hatched later will moult more quickly and start dropping their feathers at 6–8 weeks old. In November the Fifes bred later will be smaller than the first round birds and could make better show birds but they will continue to grow and reach the same size as earlier birds after the show season.

Despite myths to the contrary I have found that young birds born in September, whether they be Fifes or Goldfinches, will come into breeding condition 6 months after hatching, ready to breed the following Spring. The old birds might need to be 'encouraged' to moult, as some hens would lay a third and fourth round of eggs into August and September if allowed. This drags the breeding season on unnecessarily and the hens tend to produce clear eggs or fail to rear the young as their hormones change and they start to moult. It is natural instinct that makes a hen desert her youngsters when the season changes. In any event you want your hens fit and conditioned for next year's breeding season.

If when most of your adult Fifes have started moulting, some birds – usually hens – are trying to go on breeding, remove them from their single cages and place them at the opposite end of the birdroom, having first pulled out their tails. This will trigger the feather producing hormones and hopefully the moult will soon start. Fanciers used to place them in a cardboard box for 24 hours to trigger the start of the moult.

After several days in a new cage they can be transferred to a flight cage with the other flighted hens. There will inevitably be a little squabbling from the new arrivals with the odd clear egg laid on the floor but the moult should then be straightforward for the old and the young Fifes alike.

Feeding during the moult

It is essential to continue with a good all-round diet during this period for both young and adults. Continue to provide

- good basic canary mixtures.
- regular greenfood in the form of broccoli, spinach, watercress and so on.
- the condition seed mixture.
- softfood with the liquidised carrot (for colour), kiwi fruit, apple and broccoli.
- extra charcoal, grit and cuttlefish bone.
- wildfoods – this time of year there is an abundance of wildfoods to be collected and these are enjoyed by the young Fifes. Soft green dock seeds are available towards the end of June, plantain (rat's tails), shepherd's purse, meadowsweet, plus the perpetual spinach

which goes to seed in late summer and, if given in sprays, is eagerly relished. Seeding grasses are also available in abundance and these are also relished. A further alternative is to grow black rape seed in a growbag.

Fanciers used to offer their birds linseed tea. Linseed is reputed to put a shine on a bird's plumage and is offered mixed in their softfood. Similarly, horse breeders provide handfuls of linseed to give a sheen to their coats.

First-round youngsters enjoying seeding dock at the end of June.

Simply place a spoonful of linseed in a small cup and add boiling water. Allow this to stand until next day, strain off the linseed (which can be fed to the wild birds) and use the 'tea', which is like a thin jelly, to moisten your softfood.

Soft green vegetable matter, such as Savoy cabbage, spinach leaf, beet, watercress, chinese leaf and curly kale are ideal supplements when available. Many can be grown easily and supermarkets also offer a first class selection for most of the year. Apple should be offered at least once a week as it contains natural sugar and a different fibre for the birds.

Most of these additional foods are best given each day, or when the fancier can obtain them easily. Softfood should be fed daily. Too many fanciers are hung up on, say, greenfood twice a week, softfood three times a week, extra vitamins once a week, and so on. Try to keep bird husbandry simple. I do not think any of the above foods can be given too often and the birds know what to choose. I give mine broccoli florets every day and they attack them just as vigorously each day! The only foods to watch are the seeds containing a high proportion of fat.

At this time of year stop giving them a soaked seed mixture in hot weather. The young birds manage well enough on hard seed if it is given with softfood and greenfood.

Additives

The only additive I use during the moult is seaweed powder which I purchase at the National Exhibition of Cage and Aviary Birds, Birmingham. I add a handful of seaweed powder to a bucket or so of hard seed. As the Fife shells the seed most of the seaweed powder is removed by the tongue. This is an invaluable source of natural vitamins and minerals.

Many years ago when I bred Red Factor Canaries I used to add Parrish's Chemical Food to the drinking water as it was supposed to 'fix' the colour in birds. Boots now produce a similar iron and vitamin tonic which would be beneficial at this time of year. If additives such as multi-vitamins are offered then only half the recommended dosage should be given, as the birds will be getting most of their requirements from their diet. Moulting Fifes, particularly the flighted hens, will benefit from such a tonic.

This topic is dealt with in more detail in chapter 11.

Baths
At this time of year offer baths as frequently as you can but try to clean out the cages a day or so after bathing. Ideally the young birds should be offered a bath each day but I can only manage to bathe my birds and clean out their cages once a week. They still thrive because of my feeding regime throughout this period.

Colour feeding
The feeding of artificial colouring agents to Fifes is prohibited (Chapter 9) but natural colouring agents can enhance the colour, particularly in a yellow bird.

Each November I can guarantee that someone entering my birdroom will ask, "How do you get such colour into your birds?"

Good colour is bred into Fifes as are good feather texture and type. In other words, reject the birds that do not have the necessary colour or breed them with cinnamon and white Fifes (see chapter 11).

Having said that, colour can be enhanced quite easily during the moult.

Many years ago I went to Fife in Scotland and purchased a clear buff cock from the leading Fife fancier in the United Kingdom at that time. His birds were excellent in type and anyone wanting good, clear birds inevitably crossed his threshold. The bird was a beauty but down in colour, and I hoped the birds I bred from it would inherit colour from my own stud. He told me he never used greenfood for rearing and kept the birds in his house.

The following year I did breed some youngsters of improved colour from him but the clear buff cock himself moulted out such an extremely deep colour I could not believe it was the same bird. The difference was that, in his second moult, he had received spinach, broccoli and carrot (in the softfood) every day throughout the moult.

Carrot enhances a clear Fife's natural colour. Long before artificial colour agents like Carophyl Red were on the market, the breeders of Red Factor Canaries, as they were then known, would feed their birds on large qualities of carrot to improve the colour.

Other natural colouring agents such as red nasturtium flowers should be avoided as they tend to harden the feather, although the leaves are useful.

To give them any colour food just for a short period during the moult will result in patchiness. My Fifes are fed on carrot in the softfood from the day they hatch to the day they complete their moult. In addition, the odd African marigold flower does no harm and keeps the youngsters active.

When judging I have occasionally seen Fifes that had been fed on artificial colouring agents during the moult. The feathers were extremely hard, spoiling what would have otherwise been a good exhibition bird.

Natural foods are always beneficial during the moult: unsprayed chickweed (if any remains), green seeding dock, seeding grasses and plantain are easily collected in quantity and fed to the young Fifes who, because of their inquisitive nature, will sample anything.

Since the introduction of Carophyl Red for Colour Canaries, Carophyl Yellow has come on to the market to improve the yellow ground colour of other varieties of canary. There is no reason why new fanciers should not experiment with this colouring on Fifes that are not going to be exhibited.

It is difficult to dissolve the Carophyl Yellow in water. I found that the only way to achieve success (with Carophyl Red for Bullfinches) was to place just a few grains in a jug and add a few tablespoons of cold water. Allow this to stand overnight, after which boiling water can be poured on to it and the liquid is ready to be placed in tubular drinkers once it has cooled down.

Stuck in the moult

Some fanciers admit to having Fifes that never complete their moult, particularly the birds bred later. For that reason I only take eggs in April, May and June, so that even the later bred birds complete their moult during October.

If an old bird, or even a youngster, appears to be struggling to finish its moult it is probably out of condition or possibly ill. I would suggest the treatment I also recommend to kick start a broody hen: place the bird in a new single cage in another part of the birdroom and reduce the amount of daylight by placing a newspaper or cover over the front of the cage. Continue to provide good food mixtures, particularly granulated charcoal and, in case the bird is ill, put it on a mild solution of antibiotics for 6 days.

End of moult

During September I add sunflower oil to the dry seed mixture in place of the seaweed powder. This oil is the easiest natural vegetable oil to digest and I feel it completes the sheen on the feathers and is simpler to administer than linseed tea. Once again, small measures are called for. I apply half a cupful to a bucket of dry seed and mix the seed well by hand. Allow the mixture to soak overnight and then give it to the birds. Continue with this over the next few weeks.

Tips

1   Do not wean the young Fifes too soon. Make sure they are picking up from the floor before they are removed from their parents. Quartered apple can save a chick's life as it contains moisture and natural sugars to sustain a young bird at this stage of its development.
2   Never place newly weaned babies in a cage with perches.
3   Try to keep the youngster's feet clean; otherwise they will perch and eat old food and excrement stuck to their feet. Remember to clean the perches at the same time.
4   The deep coloured youngsters are the cocks, whether of yellow or buff feather type. This is more noticeable on the throat.
5   Aim for a quick, healthy and clean moult by leaving the birds in the same flight cage over the summer, practising strict cleanliness and providing an adequate diet for feather growth.
6   Overcrowding can cause feather plucking and other mischief. If this is happening, tie pieces of hessian string to the cage front or alternatively provide bunches of seeding grasses regularly.
7   Ensure that young birds have plenty of fresh air, without draughts, throughout the moult. Offer baths as often as possible.
8   Once the last youngsters have been weaned, clean out all empty breeding cages, spray with Johnson's Anti-Mite or similar and hang a new Vapona block in the birdroom to deter mites.
9   Handle the birds as little as possible during the moult. Treat it as a rest period before the activity of the training and show season.
10 Any youngster sat on the floor with its wings down and narrow eyed is very ill, probably with enteritis or 'going light'. See Chapter 13 for treatment.
11 *The secret of success:* greenfood, greenfood, and greenfood.

Chapter
Eight Show Training and Retention of Stock

Early Training

Towards the end of July many of the first-round Fifes will be coming through the moult and some will be exhibiting show potential. Some fanciers start to train their young birds of around 6 weeks old. This is fine if you have the time but at this stage the rearing of the second-round youngsters requires a great deal of effort. It is easier to wait until August or even September to start training in earnest. To make the task easier, once I have filled my first three flight cages with about 60 youngsters around mid-July I start to hang my training cages (similar to but slightly larger than show cages) on to the flight cages to get the birds used to running in and out of them at will.

Encourage the young Fifes to run in and out of the training cages, without removing the cage. This is easily done by placing condition mixture in the plastic drinkers on the training cages so that the birds go in to get a titbit. Hanging watercress, chickweed or other greenfood from the top of the training cages also encourages them in. This gives them total confidence in the training cages as they see them as places where certain goodies are available.

I place kitchen roll on the floor of the training cage and change it daily but a sprinkling of cat litter on the paper will absorb the droppings so that the paper can be changed every 2–3 days if time is at a premium.

Training cages hung on flight cages. The youngsters are enticed in by watercress.

Roy Fox prefers to use mixed or oystershell grit on the floor of the training cages, which keeps both the perches and the birds' feet clean. The birds then spend more time on the perches, not on the floor as they do when trying to destroy paper towels.

As a further safety measure, softfood could be offered from now onwards only in the training cage, so that any spillage could be removed every day.

Selecting Exhibition Stock

By the end of August most young Fife canaries will be through the moult with only the head feathers to come through (denoting adult plumage) and the final gloss to be put on the youngsters' new feathers.

It is difficult for anyone to predict accurately at this stage which Fifes are possible National winners as the youngsters change shape so frequently during the moult. Many appear slightly over-large but, when the feathers are complete, they are of a good pear-shape and diminutive size. Others look like world-beaters at 4 weeks of age but 'run away' at the later stages. That is why exhibits that will do well at the early shows occasionally fail to do well later in the season.

As the fancier improves the quality of his or her stud over the years, the final selection gets more and more difficult as there is less to choose between the birds. At this stage the

Selecting the youngsters to keep and show in September.

task cannot be undertaken until the Fifes have moulted out completely. That is why, these days, I do not even look in too much detail at my young Fifes until September when I remove them from their moulting flight cages.

The moult takes more out of the birds and is much longer than is often realised. It will take some birds 3 months to complete their moult, although the later bred birds will take a little less.

After a few weeks, or in my case 2 months when I start training in September, the Fifes are very confident running in and out of the training cage, so the transition from this gentle training to full training is simple.

As I have 24 training cages I run the first flight of youngsters into them, one to a cage, and leave them for a few minutes to let them settle. I usually choose a sunny Saturday or Sunday to carry out this task as the young Fifes love being placed in the sun. Most will sunbathe for a while but then start to move around and call to the other young Fifes.

I leave them for 15–20 minutes to assess their potential and then run them back into their flight cage. Do not spray them at this stage but continue with their regular baths.

Run the next crop of youngsters from the next flight into the training cages and repeat the process until all the first-round youngsters have been assessed. Do not make any rash decisions at this stage: it is too early to decide, particularly if you have a solid stud.

Each year I breed 20 or so heavily variegated or self green yellow hens, all of a similar type. I do not let any go until the end of October, by which time I am reasonably sure which ones to retain.

These days most of my Fifes take to being alone in a training cage like ducks to water, particularly after having the freedom of the cage for several weeks. Any young bird that panics in the cage at this stage should be returned to the flight cage after a few minutes if it does not settle. If it still panics the next time it is run into the training cage it will not make a good show bird as it will not have the composure to stand up to vigorous scrutiny by a judge. Any bird that does not appear confident in the show cage should be discarded from the show team and possibly even the breeding programme. Temperament, like visible exhibition qualities, is inherited. Nervous birds cannot show themselves properly or be judged accordingly. Competition these days is very fierce and such a bird would have little chance of doing well on the bench. However, many novice birds show a wildness at the early shows which is due to lack of proper training.

Cage singly

After the young Fifes have been run out in their training cages over several days it will be easy to assess which will be the best show birds. These should now be housed in single cages. I try to do this 6 weeks before my first show so that any missing feathers have time to grow back.

The show birds can now be given daily training of half an hour in a show cage, with water replacing the seed in the drinkers and kitchen roll tissue still placed on the floor. Position the cage on a window sill or shelf about 1.7m from the ground, similar to a judge's staging.

After a few days, training can be increased to an hour a day until the bird will jump into the show cage as soon as it is presented at the cage door. A few days before the first show, run your birds into their show cages and then place them in their carrying box and take them for a little walk in the garden. Carrying boxes look like little coffins with handles on top, and are designed to house four to six show cages in transit. They tend to be about 1m long by 30cm high by 30cm wide (3ft x 1ft x 1ft) but they do vary.

Be particularly careful with this exercise and place the lid down to the last few centimetres before closing it completely when the youngsters are on the perches. Otherwise they will not be able to grip whilst travelling and this may cause damage or shock.

Once a bird has become totally confident in a show cage it will begin to move across the perch correctly in a jaunty manner and at an angle of 60° to the perch to show itself off correctly. Some birds lie across the perch, which tends to pull the shape and cause the wings

to stand off the body. A good method of correcting this tendency is to take them in their show cage and hang them on a clothes line in the birdroom (or in the garden on a nice day) for their hourly training session. Their movements will rock the cages gently on the clothes line causing them to grip the perch more firmly and so begin to stand at the correct angle. If your birdroom is rather small or you do not have sufficient room to do this, place cardboard around the show cages so that the birds have to raise themselves up on their legs to see over the top.

Steadiness in the show cage is the most important feature of a good Fife. A bird can change shape in seconds if it is unsettled. In addition to lying across the

One of the author's clear buff cocks nearing the end of the moult and showing excellent colour.

Hen Fifes enjoying the winter sun. Only do this when you are in constant attendance.

perch at an angle, which is useless for showing, it can draw in its feathers to appear long and thin and thus be put down by the judge before it has a chance to show its true quality.

The bird must be calm to show off its other qualities. Some birds look different in a show cage from in their flight cages and this is down to temperament. Some appear short and lacking neck, while in a show cage they have the perfect shape; others appear ideal until run into a show cage when they pull themselves slightly, giving the impression of a long, thin bird which would be quickly rejected.

General Care

Spraying

During the moult, particularly in July and August, the youngsters should be offered baths several times a week. During September the baths can be reduced and replaced by a daily light spray of warm water for a couple of seconds. This will make the bird preen every day and put a sheen on the bird's plumage.

There is no need to get the birds soaking wet as I have seen some fellow British bird fanciers do: a couple of seconds of a fine spray mist is sufficient. Sprays that are advertised for garden use are ideal for this purpose.

Add a drop of baby shampoo to the water or, preferably, a teaspoon of Johnson's Plume Spray or similar which will add a lustre to the plumage. This process should continue up to 2 days before the show when spraying can stop to allow the natural oils to show through.

The daily spray has a calming effect on the birds at this time of the year. The first time I spray the young Fifes I run them out into their old show cages and then run them, one at a time, into the training cage I use for spraying. If you spray them in their single cages the excess water might cause food or seed to go off. I select a nice warm morning so they have time to recover and dry out.

I add hot water to a teaspoon of TCP and a couple of drops of glycerine. Another time I will add the hot water to a teaspoon of witch hazel which cleans the birds if they are a little grubby. The water might appear hot but the birds are to receive a very light, fine spray for a couple of seconds only from a distance of three feet. As they get used to this the amount of spray can be increased slightly and the distance reduced.

Spraying will enhance the bird's sheen and plumage, but no amount of spraying will turn an average bird into a show bird.

Slip claw

Occasionally a young Fife will not be able to grip the show cage perch properly due to a stiff hind claw. This is known loosely as *slip claw*, and is caused by the rear toe going straight backwards rather than curling around the perch.

Genuine slip claw is when the rear toe goes forward with the front three and can be spotted soon after the chick is weaned. I usually get one young Fife with this trouble each year, but it is easily remedied. Pull the toe back and push the toe nail between the leg and the plastic ring. Holding the claw in this position until the young birds are sorted out for retention or selling will solve the problem.

Fanciers differ as to whether the stiff hind claw is hereditary or caused by an accident. I do not think it matters as there are so few of them. Like genuine slip claw, it is cured reasonably easily over a few weeks. The trick is to get the bird to develop the muscles of the feet so that it can grip properly. Remove one of its perches and replace it with a smooth metal rod (similar to a knitting needle) placed at 45° so that it runs down to the bottom of the cage at the back. This way the bird will slip down the perch, working the rear toe to retain its balance. If tubular drinkers are used, place the drinker next to the metal perch so that the Fife will have to use it.

Show cage carrying box used and recommended by the author and supplied by Bird Breeder Supplies, Howden.

The show team

By October the young Fifes selected as the show team should be housed in single cages and spending an hour a day in a training cage or normal show cage. After the hour put the young bird back into a different single cage. That way it will not become accustomed to the same cage. Until the bird has been out to a couple of early shows it needs to have its confidence developed by being moved around and placed in different cages. Place the show cage in a different position each time the bird is trained.

At this time of year encourage other people into the birdroom to get the birds used to different people, and create a little noise by leaving the radio on all day.

The first canary shows are usually held in early October and the specialist Fife shows from late October onwards.

Many fanciers state they can spot winners the day they

Youngsters well through the moult in training cage at 3 months old.

leave the nest and on the odd occasion this is true but, with a variety where so much emphasis is put on size and colour, this is difficult and shortsighted.

Many of my winners have appeared from nowhere. I have been preparing a show team for the early shows when suddenly in November I have spotted a bird bred in the second round that has gone unnoticed. This happened to me some years ago when, as I was selecting my clear yellow cocks a few days prior to the North of England Club Show, I spotted a bird that had hatched on the 12 July and was in a flight with other late bred birds just completing their moult. After a quick course of show training, this bird was placed first in a quality class of more than 30 clear yellow cocks. Two weeks later the bird was best exhibit in show at Doncaster and, the following week, was second to James Moffat's exhibit at the National Show in a large clear yellow cock class.

This bird only went to the three shows and performed extremely well despite the fact that it had never been in a show cage until mid-November. However, such birds are the exceptions which bend the rule: in general, show preparation is started in September.

By the end of October the Fifes will be properly through the moult particularly if that month has had a few cold nights to finish off the plumage. Some birds will be through sooner, particularly those bred early in the season using artificial light and heat.

Retention of stock

At the end of the breeding season the Fife fancier needs to decide which of his flighted birds he is going to retain for the following breeding season. This is usually determined by:

- the number of Fifes to retain each year so that half will be flighted and half unflighted.
- the quality of the old birds.
- the breeding success of the birds.

If your normal breeding programme contains four clear yellow cocks and four clear buff cocks, for example, then two flighted birds of each should be retained.

The cock birds that did well on the show bench last season will normally be retained. However, if one of the other cock birds bred well and produced half a dozen youngsters, all of show quality, then he should be retained at the expense of one of the better show birds if that Fife did not breed well or only produced average youngsters.

The birds which produce the winners should be retained. It is estimated that only 10% of youngsters bred are of high show quality so the birds who produce these in numbers are essential in the birdroom. No canary fancier, of whatever variety, has 100 'world beaters' in his shed. He may have half a dozen or, in the case of the leading Border Canary men, 20 or more, but these are out of up to 200 that have been bred.

On that basis, we have decided which two older clear yellow cocks to retain. We then run the young clear yellow cocks into training cages and select the best two for retention. This should be relatively easy as the best birds will now be in single cages. Judge them as you would at a show – from above, looking for type, quality and so on – but check the parentage at the same time. If the son of the clear yellow cock who produced eight show birds came third or fourth in your order then that bird should be retained at the expense of the bird you judged first, if the first bird's siblings were very average. In other words, keep small families of Fifes that have bred overall quality for development.

Each year in late October I carry out this process. The most difficult class to decide upon is the heavily variegated/self-green yellow hens. Up to 20 hens will be judged by me no sooner than mid-October (with the very late bred ones still in their flight cages). I am probably looking for the best four birds as I will retain four flighted birds.

Out of the best six or so I check the parentage and select the four that are part of a family of good birds. This might mean that the best two will go elsewhere. An old friend of mine, Gary Pearson, who for a while was Chairman of the North of England FFCC, had problems with the concept as he could not understand why I was letting birds better than the ones I was keeping go to fellow fanciers. I felt that the two birds I was letting go would not produce youngsters the following year as good as those produced by the four I had retained.

Chapter
Nine The Model

The ideal model of the Fife Canary has been illustrated in the paintings that enhance this book. These paintings however are only one-dimensional: the movement of the Fife cannot be captured in a painting. It is the movement and overall round appearance when viewed from all angles that give, the Fife its real beauty.

If the Fife was not judged from all angles, just one-dimensionally, then it would be easier to exhibit in the sort of show cage used for British birds, which has a wire front only, with the back, top and sides solid.

The Fife canary falls into the category of *type* canaries, along with the Border, the Norwich and the Yorkshire. This standard is measured primarily by the *outline* of the bird from all angles as against *colour* as in the new Colour Canaries or *song* as in the Roller canary. For instance, it is the shape of the bird that determines it is a Fife rather than a Gloster canary, although the species are of similar size.

Fife Canary Scale of Points

In type canaries, different aspects of the shape are given varying prominence and allocated points accordingly. For example, the body is allocated more points than the legs. The legs are subject to less variation and can be improved upon only very minimally, while the bodies of Fife canaries vary considerably and can be improved by selective line breeding. A scale of points has been drawn up to accommodate the main outline and qualities as follows:

Head	10	Position and Carriage	10
Body	10	Tail	5
Wings	10	Colour	10
Legs	5	Health	5
Plumage	10	Size	25
		Total	**100**

Head

When examining the standard it is sensible to start with the head. It should be small, neat, round and about the size of a marble. The ideal bird has a nice rise above the beak (which should be fine and small) and eye, forming a semi-circle from the back skull to the shoulder. It should also have a good breadth of skull and well filled-in cheeks. The eye should be as central as possible, although it will always be nearer the front of the head. When viewed from the front it should also appear round, with full cheeks below the eye. Since it is a diminutive breed of canary, a free neck is essential. This is probably the most difficult feature to perfect in the overall shape – the head should be distinct from the body, identifying it from a Gloster canary or a Robin for example, as these do not have clear and distinct necks.

Body

The body should be compact, nicely rounded and without corners. Following the line from the back of the skull, the back should start with a gentle rise over the shoulder, reaching its highest

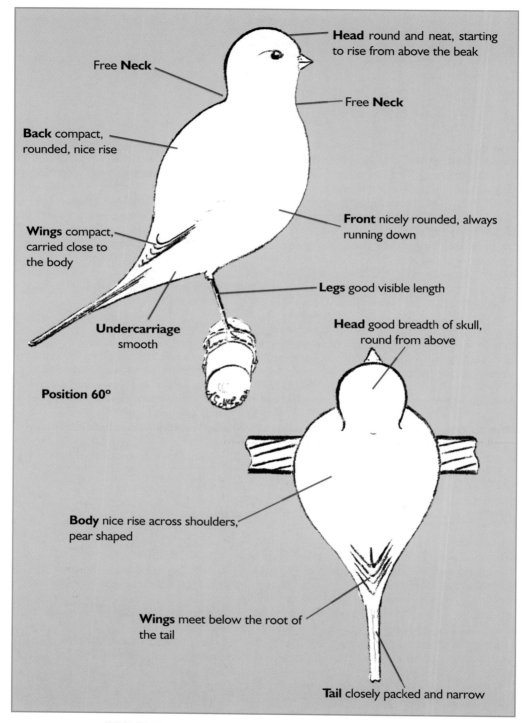

Head round and neat, starting to rise from above the beak

Free **Neck**

Free **Neck**

Back compact, rounded, nice rise

Front nicely rounded, always running down

Wings compact, carried close to the body

Legs good visible length

Undercarriage smooth

Head good breadth of skull, round from above

Position 60°

Body nice rise across shoulders, pear shaped

Wings meet below the root of the tail

Tail closely packed and narrow

REQUIREMENTS OF THE FIFE FANCY CANARY MODEL

point at the top of the shoulders and then forming a gentle curve down to the start of the tail. Similarly, the curve should run across the back from side to side. Too many birds lack this back curve; many others lack the breadth. Both features are essential and give the Fife a nicely proportioned, compact, egg-shaped body viewed from the side or pear-shaped from above. Some birds have the highest rise too low down the back, or the curve rises over the shoulders but flattens well before the tail.

The chest should be nicely rounded and the outline on the front of the Fife should always run down from the beak to the tip of the tail. Far too many birds are too prominent on the chest and the line is then forced to run upwards under the vent to the tail, giving them boat-shaped fronts; others have a 'corner' at the point of the chest, which spoils the outline. Aim to have the back and chest curves virtually equal.

The undercarriage (from the legs back to the vent) should be smooth and symmetrical. Any sign of drooping or untidy feathers ('dropped trousers') is a fault and spoils the smooth outline of the bird.

The Fife's body should always be viewed in three dimensions to ensure the overall egg or pear shape – from the side, from above and from the front. All views should show a nicely proportioned bird curving outwards from the head then tapering away to the tail.

Wings
These should be compact and carried close to the body, meeting at the tips just below the root of the tail. Poor wings ruin a good Fife as they spoil the smooth outline.

Legs
The legs should be straight, firm and in proportion to the rest of the body. They should not be too short like a Swallow's or too long like a Stilt's, but in proportion like a finch-type bird. They should appear to be at the correct angle, supporting the bird comfortably. Narrow birds have this weakness emphasised if they are too long in the leg.

The legs should also show a little thigh and be clean, free from loose scales and dainty. The bird's feet should be dainty and in proportion to the diminutive breed. Ideally they should have no loose scales, but flighted birds tend to have scaly feet to a limited extent. Although a small fault, this can spoil the overall quality of the bird.

Plumage
The feathers should be fine in quality, firm and carried close to the body, with a smooth, glossy finish. There should be no signs of roughness or hardness. Excess of feathers should also be avoided, particularly around the vent and legs.

Position and carriage
The correct position is all-important if a Fife is to show itself at its best. The bird should stand semi-erect at an angle of approximately 60° (the hands on a clock at 'five to five'). This angle is vital to the shape of the bird as to alter it exaggerates or creates other faults: wings are raised, the bird pulls itself across the perch, the tail is dropped or overall roundness is lost. Too many birds (particularly those with heavy front faults) lie across the perch and spoil the line. This is either a bad fault or due to lack of training (see chapter 8).

The procession through the perches should be smooth and confident, particularly in cocks. The head should be held high throughout the movement and the bird should have a confident and lively look without racing between the perches.

The Fife is more subject to 'wildness' in the show cage than other canary breeds but this fault can often be overcome by good training. Birds that fail to overcome the problem should be rejected from the show team and, in extreme cases, from the breeding programme.

Tail

The tail should be closely packed, narrow, nicely rounded at the tip and filled in at the root. Although the tail itself only carries a few points, a poor tail can spoil the overall shape of a bird. It should be narrow like a pipe stem, hence the term *piped tail*.

Colour

With the exception of canaries bred purely for colour, the Fife has the best and most natural colour of all the modern breeds. Clear yellow cocks should be a beautiful deep buttercup shade. It should be rich, yet soft and pure with an even tint throughout. This natural colour can be spoiled by additives, giving the plumage a hard appearance. Buffs, particularly cocks, should have a good colour in addition to a limited amount of frosting, particularly on the head and breast. The best coloured buff cocks are those that need a second look on the show bench when viewed from the front to ensure they are not yellows.

Good colour is bred into a bird and any birds with poor / lemon coloured plumage should be rejected from the clear and variegated breeding programme and show team, but they have a place in the green and white ground programme, as will be discussed in Chapter 11.

The beak and legs should match the colour of the bird: in other words, a clear bird should have light coloured legs and beak whereas a self-green bird is improved by dark legs and beak.

When looking at colour and comparing cocks with hens and yellows with buffs it is important to compare like with like. A yellow cock will have a decided advantage over a buff hen, and this should be fully taken into account when awarding points. (For illustrations of the various colours, see pages 93-102)

Health

Birds should not be exhibited unless they are in good condition and can stand the strain of a show, particularly a 2-day show. To allocate points to health alone could be seen as a waste of points, as no bird in poor condition should appear on the show bench. However, the cleanliness of the bird, particularly of its feet and its show cage, could carry due weight if the judge is faced with two exhibits of roughly equal standing.

Size

The size of an exhibition Fife should be approximately 11cm (4¼in) in length from tip of beak to tip of tail. Unfortunately, there is no stipulated size for breadth across the shoulders, although this is regarded by leading exhibitors as being just as important as length for roundness.

The problem with stipulating categorically that a bird should not be over a certain length is that no one can actually measure the bird to check this aspect. A small, thin-bodied Fife may appear longer than a stocky bird with good shoulders and neat tail, yet the opposite might be the case. The best guide to a Fife's size is the distance between the perches in the show cage. When the bird is in the cage the end of its tail should not reach the opposite perch, even on the largest buff cocks.

Again, it is unfair to compare a buff cock with a yellow hen, as nature has deemed that the former will be larger and longer than the latter. The Fife is a diminutive breed and we are all looking for birds that have all the aforementioned qualities, yet in a miniature size.

Size is very important and for this reason it is allocated the greatest number of points. In judging, large birds might be among the first to be rejected. However, the dilemma appears when you have to judge a small bird of good quality against one marginally larger but of even better type. The decision must hinge on the extent of difference in the other qualities and the difference in size. Judges' decisions will always vary marginally on this point but a bird that is shapeless yet 11cm long should not take precedence over a slightly larger quality bird, either in the breeding room or on the show bench.

General comments

In addition to this scale of excellence of 100 points, the green, cinnamon and white ground birds need to show the correct shade of green and have the correct markings. Many a good green bird has been put back because it was a bronzy rather than a grass green, and these points are covered in chapter 11.

No matter what the colour of the Fife, it must have the type in the first place – in other words, above all else it must be a rounded bird when viewed from all angles.

Show faults

Some of the more common faults in the Fife Canary are:

Size

Even today some Fifes are too long and narrow rather than short and egg-shaped, particularly in the Novice classes. If a bird is narrow in the shoulders it will look longer than it actually is, so try to produce birds that are dainty yet have breadth across the shoulders. A big buff cock looks smaller if it has a round back and shoulders.

Body

The most common fault is a flat back. Unlike Borders, which many people now regard as 'balls of cotton wool with no wings', many modern Fifes lack the roundness of back needed to complete the exhibition Fife. Some birds have the highest rise too low down the back, or the curve rises over the shoulders but flattens well below the tail. As with Border canaries over the past 10 years, selective breeding has brought about an improvement in this aspect of the model, so many Fifes now have a good curve on the back.

Try to avoid Fifes with a crease down the centre of the breast or an untidy undercarriage, although these faults can be overcome by selective breeding.

Wildness

Although the active, inquisitive nature of the Fife is endearing for most of the year, this activity can become a major problem in a show cage. A Fife has two shapes: one when it is totally relaxed and one when it is 'wild'. In this latter condition the bird pulls itself into what appears to be a long, shapeless bird, and this is often accompanied by flapping of the wings.

Most of this can be avoided by good show training, but even the best of this variety of canary display an unsteadiness at certain times in a show cage. If a good bird is to win in competition this must be kept to a minimum or it will stand little chance when being adjudicated.

Head

The shape of the head should be as near round as possible. The eye should not be too near the beak, as this gives a 'pinched' look to the eye and spoils the whole appearance of the head. The feathering above the beak should rise almost vertically before curving high above the eye. Many good birds, mostly yellow, fail in this respect due to finer feathering and the fault is most obvious at the front of the skull.

Dark feathering also appears to emphasise this particular fault as does a 'grizzle' mark on the head.

There should also be a distinct back skull and neck to show clearly what is head and what is back.

Plumage

Fifes with poor, rough or hard feather texture have little room in the breeding programme or the show team, particularly as this is a main feature of the breed. It is most easily examined on the back from above when the bird is in the show cage.

Wings

An unsteady bird will throw its wings about and they will remain up from the body for a little while. Once allowed to settle they should be neatly folded across the back. Some birds tend to drop them. This is usually associated with buff birds, whereas yellow birds occasionally have one or both raised. Once the bird has settled on the show bench these faults must appear minimal. It is likely that narrow shoulders will create faults in the wings.

Tail

Many birds have a tail that is broad and forked and these tend to minimise the required egg shape when viewed from above. This should be avoided. Very few points are awarded for this feature but, if a bird drops its tail, this is usually through nervousness. It destroys the whole shape of the Fife if it is not immediately rectified by the bird.

A broad tail, forked like a Siskin's, tends to detract from the width of the shoulders when viewed from above and from the front of the show cage. A drooped tail is rare in itself, usually being the consequence of another fault. Too long a tail spoils the shape of the bird by making the body appear drawn out and thus losing that overall roundness.

Position and carriage

An otherwise good bird that lies across the show cage perches is useless for showing. This fault is accompanied, quite naturally, by the raising of the wings and consequently the whole shape is destroyed. The bird needs to be up on the perches, demonstrating a confident position at an angle of 60° to the perch.

Applying the Scale of Points to the Model

These are the main faults to watch out for in present day Fifes. However, the scale of points is not entirely reflected in the model.

Size

To devote 25 points to size, although essential a decade ago, gives a total imbalance to the standard of excellence we are looking for and does nothing to help present-day birds. Large birds such as were seen on the show bench several years ago have virtually disappeared at exhibition level and would certainly never be among the winners at major shows today.

Size is clearly very important in a diminutive breed, but it should not become the criterion by which all birds are judged. Some exhibitors feel that if a bird is more than 11cm (4¼in) in length it has immediately lost 25 points which cannot be made up in other areas. I find this view rather narrow-minded and liable to reduce the overall quality of the breed.

It is virtually impossible to breed a buff cock of quality that is anywhere near 11cm in length – most are nearer 13.5cm. But if its tail is well clear of the show cage perches then, all things being equal, it should not be disregarded.

It is all a question of good judgment and a feel for what is the ideal Fife, and this is not achieved overnight. At the present time, one solution would be to re-examine the scale of points and perhaps start by reducing the points for size from 25 to 10 or 15.

Type and quality

A closer examination also needs to be made on the allocation of points for type and quality.

The present judging system allocates them as follows:

The ratio on the present scale represents type as three times more important than quality. This is because of the disproportionate allocation of points for size.

Type		Quality	
Size	25	Colour	10
Body	10	Plumage	10
Head	10	Health	5
Wings	10		
Position	10		
Tail	5		
Legs	5		
Subtotal	75	Subtotal	25
Total	**100**		

To restore some balance and improve the quality and consistency of judging more in line with present day birds, I would suggest a revised scale:

Type		Quality	
Size	10	Colour	15
Body	25	Plumage	10
Head	10	Movement	5
Wings	10		
Legs/Position	10		
Tail	5		
Subtotal	70	Subtotal	30
Total	**100**		

This reduces the balance to 2:1, and also makes improvements to the two key areas in judging: roundness of body and depth of colour.

Roundness of Body

The overall curved shape we look for in modern top quality Fifes is their most important characteristic. This should be reflected in the scale of points. Placing size where it belongs would allow judges to put more emphasis on roundness and remind them why the Fife is shown in an all-wire cage.

As I have already said, the Fife is a three-dimensional bird and should be judged in that respect. How often has a judge lined up the birds and marked them from one to seven without viewing the birds from the front? This is bad practice and the Fife might as well be exhibited in a box-type show cage if we are to judge them in one dimension only.

The Fife has a beautiful pear-shaped body when seen from above and this can only be judged from the front on the show bench or on the floor when selecting a show team.

Colour

The natural colour of a Fife sets it apart from many other breeds of canary. To win at high level competition a bird (particularly a cock) must have this quality and the points allocated should reflect this. There is no excuse for inconsistency, as colour should not be subject to different interpretations.

At the present time roundness of body and natural depth of colour together are given less points than size; as the standard of Fifes will be reviewed over the next few years perhaps these points might be reconsidered.

A final thought...

A radical action would be to abolish the points system altogether. Fifes should be judged *as a whole* and a quality bird leaps out at a judge without points being allocated in bits and pieces. This is discussed in the next chapter.

Ten Exhibiting and Judging

The culmination of the year's breeding season is the preparation of a good show team of Fife fancy canaries to go to the first show in October.

There is nothing quite as satisfying as running your show team into their black, clean, shining show cages to show off the quality of the bird. No matter how well they perform at the show it is enjoyable to see your own birds staged in good condition after a summer's effort of breeding and rearing. However, nothing beats the thrill of entering a show hall and seeing one of your Fifes surrounded by rosettes as Best Birds In Show – or one of the top ones, anyway.

Novices should serve 5 years in that status before moving up into champion status, so do not be in a hurry to move into that category – enjoy and learn as a novice.

A typical specialist Fife show during judging.

Fife Classification

Every year newcomers to the hobby will be showing their Fifes for the first time, and the classifications can be quite difficult to understand.

In general, Fifes are shown at three types of show:

- *local cage bird society club shows*, which are are run for their members only.
- *open shows*, which are run by local cage bird societies but encourage birds from outside the area.
- *specialist Fife shows*, in which only Fifes are exhibited. All the specialist Fife clubs (listed on page 111) run well organised, large shows and should at least be visited by any novice.

The culmination of all the shows is the National Exhibition of Cage and Aviary Birds held at the National Exhibition Centre, Birmingham during the first weekend in December.

It is essential to visit the cage bird society shows but it is even more important to go to, and exhibit at, the major specialist shows, the largest of which is the North of England FFCC Show, held on the penultimate Sunday in November, at which well over 1,200 Fifes from all over Great Britain can be seen and compared.

There is little point in becoming quite insular (as many exhibitors do) by joining several local clubs and only attending 'their' club shows. If we do not visit the major shows we could form a misleading impression of how good our birds are. There is nothing more exciting than to see a class of, say, 30 clear yellow cocks from all parts of the country placed before a judge of the highest calibre.

It is also extremely rewarding for the judge, particularly one of stalwarts of the fancy, to look back only as far as the early 1970s when the bird was virtually unknown and see the level of quality put in front of them today. There is still a little way to go, but the top quality exhibition Fife is now very much in evidence, with further improvements to come.

There are 30 separate classes for Fife exhibits, and champions are shown separately from novices. The full classification is used at major open shows, all specialist Fife Shows and the National Exhibition. The classes are:

Clear Yellow Cock	Green Self Buff Hen
Clear Yellow Hen	Cinnamon Variegated Yellow Cock
Clear Buff Cock	Cinnamon Variegated Yellow Hen
Clear Buff Hen	Cinnamon Variegated Buff Cock
Variegated Yellow Cock	Cinnamon Variegated Buff Hen
Variegated Yellow Hen	Cinnamon Self Yellow Cock
Variegated Buff Cock	Cinnamon Self Yellow Hen
Variegated Buff Hen	Cinnamon Self Buff Cock
Heavily Variegated Yellow Cock	Cinnamon Self Buff Hen
Heavily Variegated Yellow Hen	Clear White Cock
Heavily Variegated Buff Cock	Clear White Hen
Heavily Variegated Buff Hen	Variegated White Cock
Green Self Yellow Cock	Variegated White Hen
Green Self Yellow Hen	Blue or Fawn Self Cock
Green Self Buff Cock	Blue or Fawn Self Hen

Although to the champion exhibitor these are self-explanatory, novices (and indeed some champions) have difficulty in certain classes particularly as changes to a classification occur not infrequently. For example, a *ticked* bird is sometimes put in with the *clear* and at other times placed with the *variegated* exhibits.

Definitions of terms

Clear A clear bird shall be clear, but the presence of dark flue which cannot be seen without disturbing the bird or the natural discolouration of legs and beak shall be entirely ignored.

Ticked A ticked bird shall be one with **one** mark, coverable by one new penny, on the body, or three dark feathers on the wing or tail, side by side to form a solid mark. Any grizzle mark covered by one new penny to be classed as ticked.

At the present time, unless otherwise indicated in the show schedule, all ticked birds should be exhibited in the variegated classes.

A National Exhibition winning Three Parts Dark Yellow hen (1995) bred by A F Weaver. Photo: Dennis Avon

Variegated Those birds which have other markings in addition to the clear plumage. If the bird has up to 50% of its plumage dark then it is placed in the variegated class. If however it has more than 50% then it is placed in the heavily variegated class. Birds with over 75% dark feathers are referred to as three-parts dark but they are invariably shown in the heavily variegated classes and do not warrant a section of their own.

Self A self bird shall be one having no light feathers visible. Light flue under region of vent shall not merit disqualification. Light tips to otherwise dark feathers, wherever seen, shall be counted as light marks, so that a dark bird with such features is either a foul, three-parts dark or variegated according to the extent of such markings.

Foul A foul bird is the opposite of a ticked bird, with light feathers replacing dark ones in the definition.

Similarly to the ticked birds, fouls may be linked to the self birds but where this is not indicated they should be placed with the three parts dark or, more usually, with the heavily variegated Fifes.

General After the first 16 classes, which are always the largest at any Fife show, the classification accommodates the cinnamon and white ground birds.

Any variegated cinnamon Fife, including the heavily variegated birds and foul birds, should be placed in this category. At small shows where there are no classes for variegated cinnamons, they should be placed in the variegated classes but normally at a large show this means green variegated birds.

Similarly, with the variegated white Fifes, this means the blue and white birds plus the fawn (cinnamon on white ground) and white birds. Selfs remain that throughout the classification: green, cinnamon, blue or fawn with no light feathers.

The major shows often have several flighted classes for one-year-old birds. These tend to vary and sometimes rather irrationally have cocks and hens or yellows and buffs in the same class. Read the classification very carefully.

Colour in the definitions

The self or foul birds, just like the clear, variegated and three parts dark, must conform to the Standard of Excellence with regard to type and quality. Poor or bad colour should be penalised just as it is in the Clear and Variegated sections.

Green The correct colour shall be a rich, pure green and should be likened to grass or the top side of a young holly leaf (yellow green) and the underside of a holly leaf (buff green). Colour should be pure and level throughout, free from bronze, brown or olive tints. Pencilling on the back and flanks particularly in the hens should be dark, in harmony with that on the back. Beak, legs and feet to be dark, but failure in this respect does not lead to disqualification, but simply counts against the bird, according to the extent.

Cinnamon The correct colour to be a rich deep cinnamon throughout. The buff cinnamon to be a softer shade. Back and flank markings as with the greens, but of a brown shade and fainter. Greenish or light tints to be avoided.

Blue The correct colour to be as clear a shade of blue as possible in the yellow feathered bird. Of softer shade in the buff form. Other points as for the greens.

Fawn Colour to be a soft pinkish fawn. Otherwise as for the cinnamons.

Preparation for the Show

The young Fifes, having been sprayed regularly leading up to the first shows, should now be in first class appearance.

Hand washing the exhibits

Some fanciers like to hand wash their birds, and the fuller-feathered varieties of canary such as the Norwich may well need this treatment to compete at the highest levels. With the Fife, particularly in these days of cleaner air, this is not really necessary unless the birds have moulted in an outdoor flight.

A National Exhibition winning White Fife (1997) bred by Alan Fox. Photo: Dennis Avon

The process is quite simple if carried out smoothly and if the bird is used to being handled and has had regular sprays of warm water. Any bird that is removed straight from an aviary and washed by hand might die from shock or heart failure.

When washing a dirty bird it is best to have two basins of warm water (the second basin with a few drops of vinegar added to it), a good quality shaving brush and a bottle of baby shampoo.

Hold the bird chest down in the left hand and wash it as follows:

1   Apply the shampoo to the wet shaving brush and brush it well into the back and top of head feathers.
2   Spread the wings out on a flat surface such as the sink top and brush the feathers outwards.
3   Repeat this action for the tail.

4   Give the breast a light wash by turning the bird over in your hand on to its back.

5   Rinse the shaving brush in clean warm water.

6   Brush the soapy water out of the feathers with the clean shaving brush.

7   Rinse the bird in the first and second basins – the vinegar in the second neutralises the oil in the shampoo if any is remaining. Do not submerge the bird totally in the water and be careful to keep the nostrils well above the water level.

8   With your hand wipe off all the excess water, particularly in the wings and tail.

9   Wrap the bird in nappy lining fabric like a sausage roll and place it in front of the fire – not too near.

10   After 10 minutes or so remove the fabric, place the bird in a show cage lined with kitchen roll and place it in a quiet spot in a warm room.

11   After the bird has dried out naturally place it back in its cage.

12   The next day give the bird a light spray to which has been added a drop of baby oil.

The Dewar cage

The final preparation for the show is the show cage. I take particular pride in preparing show cages as I feel that if an exhibit is worth showing it must be presented in the best possible circumstances. Show cages should be painted every year or so and washed after every show. Old show cages can be used for training purposes.

Perhaps it should be reiterated here that the only acceptable show cage for the Fife is the Dewar show cage. It is made from 16-gauge wire with spars half an inch apart with a black gloss finish.

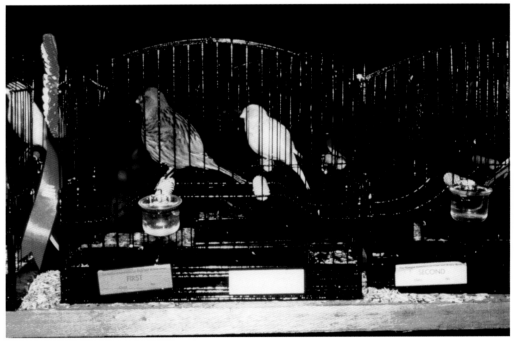

One of the author's Self Green Yellow cocks at a leading show.

The specification of the Dewar cage is as follows:

- **Overall length:** 309mm (12³/₁₆in)
- **Width:** 107mm (4¹/₄in)
- **Height:** 279mm (11in) at the centre, 228mm (9in) at each end
- **Base:** 2.4mm (³/₃₂in) thick
- **Bottom rail:** 35mm (1³/₈in) x 4.7mm (³/₁₆in)
- **Corner posts:** 310mm (8¹/₄in) long x 4.7mm (³/₁₆in) square
- **Drawer front:** 25mm (1in) x 19mm (³/₄in)
- **Handle:** 12.7mm (¹/₂in) round head screw
- **Drinking hole:** 22mm (⁷/₈in) x 19mm (³/₄in)
- **Crossbar:** 114mm (4¹/₂in) from base
- **Frame:** 16 gauge wire
- **Filling:** 18 gauge wire
- **Finish:** black gloss

Dewar cages can be purchased from most avicultural specialists, as can special Fife show cage perches. Secondhand ones are also often available and can be washed and repainted to an acceptable level.

These show cages are sometimes referred to as Border show cages as they have been the standard show cage for Border canaries for many years – long before the Fife split off from the Border as a breed. When the Dewar cage was introduced the Borders were nearer to the size of present-day Fifes and the cage was tailor-made for them. Today the odd Fife fancier will suggest that the Fife should have its own show cage. It has – the Dewar! This is more appropriate to the modern Fife than to the modern Border. If any variety needs another show cage then it is the Border now they are larger. However, I think the Dewar suits both varieties, and this is convenient as many fanciers keep both Borders and Fifes.

Before a show the preparation of the show cage is important. All cages should be sprayed with black paint at least every third year. A fine spray is sufficient to retain that nice gloss. Regular washing and wiping over with a touch of turpentine puts a good shine on the paintwork.

When you re-assemble a Dewar show cage, make sure that the perches are correctly positioned – one perch on the drinker wire and five clear wires before the next perch.

Make sure the drinkers fit properly into their supporting wires. Drinkers need to be supported at the correct height and should be held level rather than sloping. If a drinker slopes away from the cage, water can spill everywhere when it is filled, and it could be difficult for a bird to reach the water. Drinkers should be cleaned after each show.

Carrying boxes need to be well cleaned out and an anti-mite preparation should be sprayed into the corners. Then leave the lid open for a few days to let the air get in.

You are now ready to pack a few cages into the boxes, to give your Fifes their first experience of a carrying box.

Make sure that each bird is on the perch and close the carrying box lid. Then rock the box gently backwards and forwards so that the bird grips the perch firmly and does not flap around. Carrying the box around the garden helps to steady a bird, ready for when it goes to a show.

It is also important to make sure, well before the show, that your carrying boxes fit snugly into your car. It does the birds no good at all if they travel to the show in boxes that are tipped up at an angle, fall down or will not fit into the boot or on the back seat of your car.

Finalise the preparation of your show cages several days before the show date. Place the clean perches in the cage, leaving five spaces between them, and place the first one on the small wire below the drinking hole. Stick the labels on the bottom rail of each cage with the middle of the show cage label directly beneath the perch wire not holding the drinker.

Keep a record of the cage label numbers for easy identification at the show and mark these numbers in pencil on the front of the cage so that the bird can be put back in its own cage on return.

Next, sprinkle oat husks on the floor of the show cage. Firstly lightly spray the bottom of the cage; next sprinkle plain canary seed on the floor and then the oat husks. This holds the oat husks in place. Otherwise, being very light, they can move around the bottom of the cage in transit and spill out, as well as covering the seed in the hopper. Alternatives have been discussed such as corrugated cardboard or blotting paper on the show cage bottom, but oat husks are highly absorbent, help to keep the birds' feet clean, and also look far more natural.

Some fanciers find it difficult to obtain oat husks but they are always available, along with glass drinkers, from John E Haith Ltd.

Finally fill the seed hopper with canary seed. Make sure you take enough show cage drinkers, plus a couple of spares, to the show.

Final Preparation

Wherever possible it makes sense to take the Fifes to the show hall the evening before the show. This gives the birds plenty of time to settle down before the adjudication. If they are taken there in the morning the clear yellow cocks, being the first class, may only have a few minutes to settle down in a new environment.

At this time check the condition of the birds' tails and feet. Dirty feet can spoil a good bird's chances at a show as can a dirty tail and these should be washed thoroughly. It is also a good plan to 'pipe' the tail of the Fife at this stage by bending the two halves inwards after washing. Any broken feathers should be removed.

Once the birds are in place, place them in the carrying boxes and close the lid to within 2–3cm of the box. That way the Fifes will go down to roost and the lid can be closed after a few minutes.

For some Fife fanciers the final minor point for show preparation is when the birds are placed in their carrying cages before being taken to the show hall the previous evening. They give the birds the lightest of fine sprays just prior to closing the lid; this way the birds will preen in the morning just as they would in the wild following the dew settling on their bodies during the night. This will tend to raise their feathers and give them that just-brushed look.

Carrying boxes can cause more problems than might at first be apparent. Unless they are uniform it can take ages trying to find which cage fits into which box and all the time the birds in the cages are being disturbed. It is well worth the effort to ensure that every one of your show cages fits into every one of your carrying boxes. At the end of a show, the sooner your birds are packed into their boxes the sooner you can be on your way home – which is good for you and your birds.

Returning Home

The show team usually arrives home late in the evening. My birds tend to receive a lot of attention when they are at shows so they will have had a busy day. After a long ride home the birdroom will be in darkness so I leave it until the next morning to return them to the stock cages. Overnight, the carrying box lids are wedged open to let air in.

Once the birds are back in their own cages they are given a little condition mixture or softfood. This is excellent to help them to recover quickly from their outing.

Some fanciers offer a little brandy or sherry in the drinking water. This is another old wives' tale and should not be done as it reduces the bird's body temperature and depresses the system. Wherever possible I let the Fifes have a bath or possibly a light spray.

If your Fifes are prepared properly before they go to a show and are given every attention on their return they will not suffer from the experience.

End of the Show Season

I have always maintained that the canary management year begins the day after the National Exhibition of Cage and Aviary Birds.

The National is the culmination of the year's efforts and it is every fancier's ambition to win the top award in his particular section. Numbers are increasing every year: during the late 1970s through to the early 1990s the number increased 10-fold. In 1977 there were 68 Fifes whilst in 1991 there were 1,525 Fife exhibits.

After the National Exhibition I wash my show cages and put them away until the following show season.

Regional Variations in Quality

I have heard it said, and have said myself in the past, that there are inconsistencies in the judging of Fifes which will never be resolved.

I have also heard it said that there are different types of Fifes in different parts of the country. This is nonsense: there are simply good Fifes and poor ones. It just so happens that there are more good quality Fifes in certain parts of the country than in others.

This is particularly evident to me as, living in the north of England, I used to travel more widely than any other top exhibitor. I made a point of never missing the Scottish All-Fife Show and I invariably have a judging engagement in Ireland or Wales each year in addition to many excursions into central England.

Andy McEwan's interpretation of one of the author's winners.

I have noticed that the standards are improving, and they will continue to do so with good breeding management. There is a quality there in many parts of the country and this will only increase as fanciers are able to see Fifes of the highest standards at the National Exhibition.

When I first won the National Exhibition my own bird was chosen unanimously by what I regarded as probably the top three English judges at the time: Roy Fox, Gordon Adamson and Arthur Johnson. You might say I have an obvious vested interest in saying that but it shows that the judging of Fifes at the highest level is becoming more professional and consistent as, less than 3 weeks earlier, that particular Fife was selected as Best Fife at the North of England FFCC show out of well over a thousand birds. On that occasion I regarded the three judges in question as the top three Scottish judges at the time: James Moffat, Neil Cameron and Neil Cameron Jr.

On both occasions the quality of competition was extremely high. I had twelve firsts at the North of England FFCC show and seven firsts at the National Exhibition in the first large 16 classes. Despite this level of fierce competition, even from many of my own birds, the little buff cock's quality stood out to both teams of judges.

Those were the only two occasions that bird was exhibited. However, a Fife of that quality must be used to maximum benefit, so I carefully selected two yellow hens to pair to him for the following breeding season. One was the self green yellow hen that took firsts at our club show and the other was Best Three Parts Dark at the National Exhibition in 1988.

Judging

After 7 years as an exhibitor and member of one of the specialist Fife clubs a fancier can apply to go on to the Fife Fancy Federation list of approved judges, known as 'panel judges'. It does not matter if he or she has only served 2 years as a novice – the 7-year rule still applies.

These are the only judges allowed to judge at specialist or open shows where patronage has been awarded by the Fife fancy specialist clubs. At local cage bird society club shows (in other words, closed to outside members) any fancier can judge, so these are good events in which to gain experience. However, the best way to learn to judge is to study the model very carefully and gain experience over several years of judging your own youngsters in the autumn. Steward at shows wherever possible and watch how an experienced judge carries out his or her task. Perhaps allowing people to stay in the show hall and watch the judging is no bad idea.

For the first year or so it is useful for a novice exhibitor to get a local champion exhibitor of Fifes to sort out which birds to exhibit. Don't make the mistake of asking a judge of another variety of canary to sort them out for you.

The Fife Fancy Federation meets annually in April at Blackpool to consider, amongst many other things, fanciers who have been recommended for inclusion in the list of approved judges. Almost all are accepted as their own Fife club will be aware of their track record as an exhibitor.

Once on the list, a judge can officiate at any canary show. This is where the canary judges differ from the budgerigar judges and, sadly, it will always lead to criticism of judges' capability. In my view, the criteria for appointing judges need further assessment to avoid inconsistencies in judging.

As far as putting a fancier on to the list, I feel that 7 years is far too prescriptive and for many people too long. Over the past 20 years most of the fanciers who have joined the Fife ranks have moved over from other branches of the hobby. If that fancier is already a judge for another type of canary then clearly he will not need an additional 7 years. As Thomas Hardy

The ultimate in exhibiting.

wrote, *Experience is a question of intensity rather than duration.* In other words, some people could keep birds for 27 years and would not make panel judges. Some of this is down to confidence. On the other hand, if a top Border exhibitor and judge starts to keep Fifes, I expect him to be able to claim judge status after a year.

My other area of concern is that once an exhibitor has obtained judge status he is eligible to judge specialist shows and even have his name submitted for consideration to judge the National Exhibition.

Competent, confident judges should be developed and encouraged partly by stewarding and watching at major shows, but it is no easy task to place exhibits in order of merit down to the first 7 in a class of 50 clear buff hens, for example, now that the standards are improving all the time.

Champion breeders should be able to apply to become a judge after 4 years. Judges could be graded into A and B categories. Newly-appointed judges would be given B status and they would then be able to judge the cage bird society shows for 3 years. That way the 7 years as champion would be put to good use, by which time judging experience would be gained and they could then be placed in the A category.

Only after judging a certain number of specialist shows over a 2–3-year period should that judge be considered for judging the National Exhibition or top specialist Fife shows such as the North of England FFCC, where a judge might encounter classes of 50 or 60 good exhibits.

Remember that the judges set the standards. The better the judge, the better the standard; judges make the progress, not the model.

Judge the whole

The only correct way is to judge the Fife as a whole. A good judge quickly recognises the superiority of one exhibit over another. Why in a flight of 20 young Fifes in your birdroom does one almost leap out at you? It is that something special – roundness and cobbiness from all angles, overall quality and type. That is how Fifes should be judged. The winners at specialist Fife shows should have that type of impact.

Fifes should not be judged in bits and pieces. I know we have points for this and points for that but the worthwhile essential features stand out for themselves. Judges should recognise the superiority of one exhibit over another and place them accordingly in order of merit.

That, in my opinion, is why the United Kingdom method of judging a bird of movement like a Fife is superior to the continental method whereby birds are given points for each aspect of the bird (9 for head, 4 for feet, and so on) with a possible total of 100. That way, the top bird could end up with 87 points while an inferior bird could obtain 88 points from another judge. A couple of fellow fancier friends of mine recently judged on the continent using this method. They judged 133 exhibits and it took them from 9.00 am to 6.00 pm!

First judging engagements

The first thing to do when offered a judging engagement at a small show is to check the venue – where it is and how far away – so that you allow plenty of time to get there. These days I tend to travel the day before a major show and stay at a nearby hotel at my own expense, making the event more of an enjoyable weekend.

Many fanciers set off to specialist Fife shows at 4.00 or 5.00 am on the morning of the show. The only problem with that is the uncertainty of the weather in autumn. On one occasion when I was to judge the Southern England Fife Club Show at Little Paxton near

Cambridge I woke up to dense fog. Unfortunately, I had to turn back after a couple of hours.

A rough target for judging is 60 Fifes an hour, so knowing the number of Fifes before you start is essential. Sometimes a judge may be faced with a far greater entry than he anticipated and this must be taken into account. On these occasions it is difficult to allow every Fife all the time it might need to settle.

Check the special classes list so that you know exactly what you have to find at the end of judging: for example there might be a special for *best flighted*, *best white* or *best opposite sex*. It is useful to know this as you start to judge.

Always ensure that where you are to judge has plenty of natural light. Never face the light, and have your back to the window if possible. Make sure your trestles are set at the most comfortable height for you.

Make sure the stewards (who may be budgerigar or foreign bird fanciers) carry the show cages by holding them at the bottom and not with hands over the top, as this can cause the birds to panic. Allow the birds plenty of time to settle and then check that all the exhibits are there.

Some judges put their first prize winners on a table near to hand until all the judging has been carried out. I prefer to keep a note of the firsts worth considering for specials later in the day and return them to the staging. This is for the sake of the Fifes. The first class (usually the clear yellow cock) will be judged at say 9.30 am and the winner could then be placed at the side for several hours, subjected to stewards walking by and a lot of activity. Many a bird has gone to pieces after several hours away from the main staging. One judge I saw many years ago judged all the champion and novice birds and placed winners 'near to hand'. By lunchtime there were birds on window ledges, cupboards and anywhere he could find a ledge. Many of these birds need not have been retained and the final selections for specials was chaos!

The class must be reduced to a manageable number. The birds with discernible quality can be moved to one side of the judging table and obviously poor quality birds or wild ones can be sent back to the staging fairly quickly. Birds in this category tend to be the long birds, the ones with bad faults or weaknesses or, in the case of cock birds, those with the very poor colour which, when they are placed alongside good coloured cocks, makes them look like hens colour.

It is essential to note the weakness on the cage label. This is useful for novices and juniors as they can see several hours later what the fault was at the time of judging and also reminds the judge when he is questioned by the owner. One or two words will suffice: 'wings' when the bird is crossing its wings at the time of judging; 'colour'; 'wild'; 'soft'; or even 'dirty cage'. You will always get bad losers, even in the champion ranks, who will question your decision.

The best Fifes tend to leap out at you and your first impression of a quality bird is usually the correct one. Put the top few birds to one side of the trellis – and we have now sorted out the possible winners and rejected the poor quality birds with obvious faults.

The birds which fall between these two categories need just as careful selection as the potential class winners. In a large class of 60–70 Fifes if I find 10 good birds to hold back I will judge them down to 10 for the benefit of their owners.

Once the individual classes have been judged comes the final selection for the top awards. In a full classification it is easiest to do this as you go along. For example, once you have finished the first four clear bird classes it is best to select from those four birds one as 'best clear'. It is sensible as you have just spent some time looking at clears and you have been considering all the different features of a good clear and it is fresh in your mind; you have also just seen the four birds in question and their individual attributes.

If done sensibly the final selection is the most enjoyable part of judging. It is here that a judge must go back to the schedule to distinguish cocks from hens and give due allowance for size and colour, as these differ in the sexes as well as in yellow and buff feather types. If this were not done then yellow hens would win the top awards because of their smaller size, particularly with the present scale of points.

It is unfair not to give due weight to buff cocks of quality, particularly the darker birds that are not as eye-catching. You must compare like with like and weigh accordingly.

When I judged in Wales recently I was faced with a good novice class of variegated yellow cocks. The best bird was of immense quality but had very poor colour. The bird was clearly a *hen* and, when I took her outside to have a closer look at her colour, she displayed the hen's 'frosting' of feather particularly around the back of the neck. I knew that the bird, although of excellent quality, would not take a top award because of this weakness. I asked the chief steward if this particular novice (obviously I did not wish to know who he was) had a bird in the variegated yellow hen class, so that he could check that those two birds had not been run into the wrong cages.

Clear yellow Fife cocks should possess a deep buttercup shade. Buff birds should also possess good colour, although of a different tone.

Buff cock birds when handled should show almost yellow colour on the breast and more obviously on the rump. This is also the case with green Fifes; in poor light, a good buff cock could appear a similar colour to a yellow hen. This happened to me at a show in Wales when I had to take a superb self green buff cock into the daylight to confirm it was in fact a buff cock.

It is good to see a buff winning major awards as it is easy for a judge to select a yellow hen because of her daintiness and size. At the final adjudication a judge needs his show classification to make an accurate decision as he is faced with cocks and hens. One cannot assess the colour or even the size aspects unless one knows whether it is a cock or hen.

Health and condition are awarded five points. This is a little superfluous as a bird that is soft is immediately sent back to the staging once the label has been noted. If the 'soft' condition becomes apparent later during judging, the bird is not judged any further. These birds cannot show off any of their features and should never be exhibited.

Size is the most important feature of the exhibition Fife, although I smile at some of the nonsense talked on this issue. Until we get buff cocks the same size as yellow hens (which is never!) judges must use a little common sense. The ideal size is 11cm (4¼in) overall length. How was that determined when the original Fifes were much longer? Given the reasons for exhibiting Fifes in all-wire show cages, why is there no ideal in overall width at the shoulders? Fifes do not have a flat image.

How do we actually measure the length of a bird which is moving to and fro? Should we never exhibit buff cocks? I have never seen one of good quality at this length?

Clearly, despite my rhetorical questions, the first and most important aspect of judging Fifes is size; after that, the roundness of body and other features play a part in the selection until we have the nearest to the ideal Fife in each class. This may not necessarily be the shortest, but will certainly be among the shortest.

It is all a question of balance and judgment based on experience. A judge or exhibitor should know how good a buff cock is compared to other buff cocks. I have always maintained that an average yellow hen will always look good to a novice, particularly a clear bird.

Fanciers should try to get away from the narrow interpretation of the size aspect of the Fife. A small Fife must have all the other qualities to win; otherwise a slightly larger bird of quality must take the top award.

Wrongly classed

Some Fifes are obviously put in the wrong class by carelessness on the part of the fancier – if for example a clear yellow cock has been run into a show cage intended for a self green. These birds need to be marked 'wrong class' and also with the class in which the exhibit should have been entered.

Other Fifes are placed in the wrong class when the fancier thought he was entering in the correct class. With the present classification these tend to be in the self classes as the foul birds are shown with the heavily variegated. My opinion is that to put the foul birds in the same class as the self green birds would remove the majority of the wrongly classed entries which, on occasions, can spoil a good class of Fifes because of the high percentage of cages marked 'w/c'.

The guidance to judges is not to wrong class *if there is reasonable doubt*. It doesn't help novices if a Fife is wrongly classed and then at a later show wrongly classed the other way. It makes sense to merge the offending classes defining the green birds' markings.

The example I have used for many years took place when I was judging the All Wales Fife Show. Tony Bell, my fellow judge and one of the leading Fife fanciers at the time, brought over a green yellow hen which went on to take a first at the National Exhibition a few weeks later. The bird was an absolute gem in every way.

Tony asked for a second opinion: did I think it was a self or should be in the heavily variegated class? As it was clearly borderline I said, "Tony, if the bird is in the heavily variegated class then it is a heavily variegated; if it is in the self class then it is a self!"

We are judging the Fife, no matter what colour or class, and birds should not be wrong classed unless it is absolutely necessary and very clear cut.

National exhibition

At some of the top Fife shows and the National Exhibition we are now seeing classes of 50–60 Fifes and at the 1998 North of England FFCC show I judged a class of 73 variegated yellow hens. This is a tall order and only a very experienced judge should be invited to place so many exhibits in order of merit in the allotted time.

Unless they are judged in blocks of 15–20 the task is easier to carry out if use is made of note-paper and pad. As the Fifes are very active little birds they change shape and position quite regularly. You can make allowances for this if you have 10

One of the author's self green yellow hens nearing the end of the moult.

Fifes on the trestle and they can all be watched and assessed.

If 60 clear buff hens are put in front of a judge then a note can be made of the few 'world-beaters' in the class and of the birds that could never make the top seven. If after watching them for a little while you are still of the same opinion, the inferior birds can be sent back to the staging. You must be doubly sure of Fifes sent back as the owner has the right to ask why the bird did badly. The class can eventually be brought down until you have selected the seven winners.

Eleven Colour and Colours

When good colour in Fifes is mentioned I immediately think of the clear yellow Border cocks my grandfather kept. I recall them as being almost orange on the head and throat when they had finished their moult. The correct definition for such birds is *buttercup yellow*.

Good colour is an essential part of a quality exhibition Fife but is often neglected by judges. Since it is part of the standard of excellence, why neglect it? Clearly the shape is more important but sound colour is essential and must be exhibited in our Fifes, particularly the cock birds.

In large classes of 40–50 cock Fifes you may find several birds with a poor colour or hen's colour. In such tough competition these birds should not be placed in the first seven. So that the exhibitor is aware of the reason I endorse the cage 'colour – hen?'

If Fife fanciers want to improve the colour of their birds then pairing a good coloured bird to a poor one can only be part of the answer. I do not recommend it– such poor coloured birds can be used in the green and white pairings.

The answer to improving colour is to **pair good coloured Fifes to other good coloured ones. Never use poor coloured cock birds in a clear line.**

Some fanciers tell novices to pair a green to a poor-coloured clear Fife to improve colour. This will not work and is dealt with under **Green Fifes** in this chapter.

To ensure good colour throughout a stud ranging from clears to greens the fancier must realise that there are two basic ground colours in modern studs of Fife canaries. The clue to this is in the variegated birds in my stud. If I breed 20 variegated Fifes in a breeding season and line them up haphazardly in show cages I will be able to tell you from a distance of 30m which were bred from my clear/variegated line and which from my heavily variegated/green line. The former have a base yellow colour of *buttercup yellow* and the latter a base colour of *lemon yellow*. It is almost as clear as putting an orange alongside a lemon.

The old books used to say of variegated birds that the green should be grass green and the yellow buttercup yellow. This is impossible genetically. My clear line produces some variegated birds and the green colour is bronzy as though a drop of orange paint has been dropped into a tin of green paint; the clear part is buttercup yellow. My dark line produces variegated birds in which the green colour is grass green with no hint of bronze and the clear part is a beautiful lemon yellow. Mixing the lines will inevitably produce bronziness in the green lines and poor colour in the clears.

Breeding for Colour

The main point to remember, and one that seems to confuse many novices, is that colour is bred into a bird and cannot be added to any significant degree. Poor coloured birds at shows are marked down, particularly cocks, but novices inform me after adjudication that the birds have had green food every day.

Some fanciers double yellow to help to bring the size down. This may result in an improvement in colour, but will also tend to make the birds appear narrower and longer because of the narrowing of the yellow feather. If this mating is carried out one year it is essential to pair any youngsters to buff birds the following year to maintain the cobbiness.

Any break from the normal yellow and buff pairing should be carried out for one year only.

Feeding for colour

If you have started with good coloured birds the majority of the young should be of good natural colour. However, it must be helped by the provision of as near natural a diet as possible during the moult. This should include the softfood it has been reared on, but in smaller quantities, right through until the moult has finished and occasionally throughout the winter months.

Greenfood is essential during the moult and a variety of vegetable matter in the diet will improve the lustre and feather texture, but it will not enrich the basic natural colour. When I used to keep British birds I would add Carophyl Red to certain species' diet and, if given correctly and at the correct strength, this would assist the colour in, say, a cock Bullfinch *if that bird already had a good colour*. The same amount fed to a poorly coloured bird would not have the same effect.

A bird with good natural colour will come through not only with a good colour but also with the right texture if fed on the natural foods it might expect in the wild throughout the moult. The poorly coloured specimens can be improved marginally but, in my opinion, are a lost cause and should be used for breeding with whites or greens as appropriate.

Vegetables can be bought through the summer or grown in a small corner of the garden. I particularly like broccoli, spinach, leaf beet (perpetual spinach) and curly kale. All these foods are relished by the birds. If you are lucky enough to be able to find watercress growing in running water then give them this. There is nothing finer for the birds during this period, although it is expensive to purchase compared to the others. Lettuce should only be given occasionally and in very small quantities as it has very little nutritional value and causes the birds to be loose in their bowel movements.

Natural foods also can be collected at this period. Chickweed and dandelion will have finished but the odd patch will spring up and these two plants are always worth collecting. Groundsel is good seed to offer but try to ensure that the plants do not have mouldy leaves – these are liable to upset the young birds.

Dock, seeding grasses and thistle will be available from June and the birds should be given as much of these plants as they will take for the few weeks they are available.

Plantains (rats' tails) are usually reliable at all stages of development but they are at their best towards the end of the moult when many other plants have finished.

Some fanciers recommend the use of African marigolds and nasturtiums to improve the colour but these should be fed sparingly, if at all, although the marigolds are safer. They might improve the colour if given in quantity but harden the feather and tend to spoil the good feather texture quality.

Some fanciers recommend putting the Fifes to moult away from direct sunlight as they feel this bleaches the feathers a paler colour.

Pairings to Improve Colour

As far as I am concerned the only pairing to improve colour is two birds of good colour together; in other words, in a clear pairing both birds should be of good, deep buttercup yellow colour. Even a good coloured clear buff hen should demonstrate this colouring through the frosting when compared with other clear buff hens.

Some fanciers will recommend the following systems of pairing to improve colour:

*   pair yellow to yellow (for one year only).
*   pair a clear Fife to a cinnamon variegated bird, which will also produce birds with improved feather.
*   pair a green to a clear bird.
*   double buff and then pair the best coloured back to yellows.

After 40 years of breeding canaries I am yet to be convinced if any of the above improves colour.

Green Fifes

As with all colours of Fifes, it is necessary to examine green birds in daylight. Fanciers who have seen me judge will know that in a poorly lit hall I take birds outside occasionally when I am making final selections. This is particularly so in the case of green birds, especially buffs, when sometimes natural light is needed to determine whether it is a nicely coloured buff green cock or a poorly coloured yellow green hen.

There are few weak coloured green birds on the show bench today and the real grass green, particularly in a yellow cock bird, is a beautiful sight. As with clear birds, poor quality birds must be discarded in favour of the real grass-green birds.

The colouring in green Fifes is reputed to get better during the first 3 years of their life but I have found older birds develop a little bronziness.

The Standard of Points is the same for the self green: first and foremost they must have the same ideal shape as the clear and variegated birds. As far as colour is concerned, the plumage should be a rich grass green colour with as little bronziness as possible. Many fanciers blame this bronziness on cinnamon blood but it could be due to poor feeding or an incorrect breeding programme. Some of the best green cocks I have had were cinnamon carriers.

The best greens are undoubtedly the yellow feathered as they can show off their rich grass green base colour. However, only 10 points out of 100 are allocated to colour, so a good bronze green bird should beat an average grass green bird.

As well as the grass green colour, exhibition birds, particularly the yellows, should have clear, distinct markings, mainly along the flanks (especially the hens) but also on the back. These are called pencilling. They should be dark, neat and clearly defined without being too broad or too narrow and should complement the base green colour. Ideally legs and beak should match the markings.

Some green Fifes these days have developed a clear mark under the throat similar to a 'pea throat' Goldfinch. These are clearly not self birds and should be exhibited under the foul category (see definitions in chapter 10).

Remember: when assessing the quality of the colour of your green Fifes with a view to improving the colour think 'buttercup' or 'lemon'.

Cinnamon Fifes

The cinnamon Fife, a beautiful bird, is a green bird minus the black pigment. Referred to in my grandfather's day as *burnished copper*, cinnamon is the only recessive sex-linked colour. In other words, with certain pairings the sex of the youngsters can be determined as soon as they are hatched. Cinnamon is the only colour that can be predicted accurately in the breeding programme.

The effect of this mutation is to remove the black pigment from the normal green bird, thus changing its colour to cinnamon, and also lightening the colour of the legs and beak and changing the eyes from black to red. This is particularly obvious at birth – as the chick develops the colour of the eye darkens until as an adult it is difficult to distinguish the eye colours.

Many fanciers breed cinnamon to cinnamon but after a few years the colour may deteriorate and the markings also tend to fade. The depth of colour can be improved by the introduction of a green bird with deep coloured markings.

If the green bird introduced is a hen, the young can be sexed at birth. All the birds with red eyes will be hens and all the dark-eyed birds will be cinnamon carrier cocks.

If the green bird introduced is a cock, all the young will be dark-eyed. The hens will be green and the cocks will be greens carrying cinnamon – in other words, one sex chromosome will be carrying the cinnamon factor but it will not appear in the feather.

The various matings involving cinnamon birds (yellow or buff feather type is irrelevant) can be outlined as follows, with the cock mentioned first each time:

1   *Cinnamon x Cinnamon* – all youngsters will be cinnamon.
2   *Cinnamon x Green* – all cocks are cinnamon carriers (visually green but capable of producing cinnamon youngsters) and all the hens are cinnamon.
3   *Green x Cinnamon* – all cocks are visually green cinnamon carriers and all hens are green.
4   *Green Cinnamon Carriers x Cinnamon* – half the cocks are cinnamon and half green cinnamon carriers; half the hens are green and half cinnamon This is my favourite pairing to retain type and quality.
5   *Green Cinnamon Carriers x Green* – half the cocks will be green but cinnamon carriers and half will be green; half the hens will be cinnamon, half will be green. The problem with this mating is you do not know whether a cock is a carrier. This is not really desirable in a breeding programme, particularly as it may be dormant in progeny for several generations.

It should also be pointed out that a hen is either a cinnamon or a green: she cannot be a carrier. In other words, only the cock Fife can produce cinnamon youngsters or green cocks that carry the cinnamon factor. A hen needs a cinnamon or carrier cock with which to breed cinnamons. The colour in cinnamon Fifes should be rich and deep with faint darker markings on the back but more particularly on the flanks.

There is much misplaced anxiety about cinnamons either popping up all over the place or ruining the colour of the greens. This is down to bad management by the fancier and not following these basic rules:

•   only use matings where you can predict with certainly what the cocks are: either cinnamon or cinnamon carriers.
•   to produce good cinnamons, prefer *buttercup* ground coloured Fifes to *lemon*. This is the opposite of the green rule. Fanciers have paired good cinnamons to their greens and

blamed the cinnamon gene. This is incorrect – it is the ground buttercup colour that is wrong when mixed with grass green.

Remember - think 'buttercup' or 'lemon'.

We have talked here about self cinnamons paired to greens. A cinnamon variegated bird can produce clear cinnamons. These have red eyes in the nest but need watching carefully as when they are weaned there will be no visible cinnamon feather by which to identify the bird as being cinnamon or normal.

White Fifes

These Fifes have a basic white colour instead of yellow and can be produced as clear, variegated (where the green is replaced by a blue colour), self (where the green is now self blue) and cinnamon variegated or self (these are a paler cinnamon colour and are referred to as fawn).

In exhibition terms these are the *white*, *blue and white variegated* and *self blue* Fifes. In addition, there is the *fawn* bird, which is the combination of white and cinnamon.

Once again, colour is important: the blue and fawn should be rich and the white as white as possible. Some birds are spoilt by having yellow in the wing butts and primaries.

In all other respects these birds should meet the standard.

What is a white fife?

All birds have a basic ground colour of white, yellow or red, irrespective of the other colours and markings they might possess. The Blackbird has a basic white ground colour, the Canary a yellow ground colour and the Red Hooded Siskin (as used in the production of the first New Colour Canaries) a red ground colour.

The white canary is not an albino. Albinos occur in all species when there is a total lack of melanin in the make-up. An albino is always pure white, the legs and beak are flesh coloured and the nails are white. However, white canaries occur when the yellow colour gene is suppressed by another gene, resulting in the production of a white canary.

Dominant whites

Newcomers will read books or articles which talk about *dominant whites* and *recessive whites*, expanding on different theories about what to pair to what. These are very confusing and the newcomer will not know what birds he or she has. The simple rule to remember is that in the United Kingdom all whites are dominants.

Breeding white ground Fifes

Some of the white birds on the show bench are a dull colour whereas others have a lovely clean appearance, reminding one of soap powder advertisements comparing wash with wash. As noted earlier, with clear birds a bird with poor colour must be discarded. In my birdroom very rarely do I produce a poor coloured bird but, whenever I do produce such a bird, I immediately think of a white ground mate.

Many years ago I would cross my white birds with my best Fifes to have this best quality throughout my stud but invariably the birds would appear dirty white and would exhibit yellow at shoulder butts and primary feathers.

People tend to get confused with whites when talking of yellows and buffs as they think the white is separate from these two forms and must be paired to a buff bird. There are yellows and buffs in whites just as there are in all other forms of birds, whether it be clear Fifes or Blackbirds on the lawn. However, they are more difficult to identify.

The best method I have found is by silhouette. Yellow Fifes have a more distinct outline than buffs, the shoulders are not as pear-shaped and the birds are smaller. This applies equally to white birds although, like the cinnamon, they appear narrower because the white feather is fine. Yellow birds are more prone to display the yellow feathering in the primaries and at the shoulders.

Follow these rules when breeding white Fifes:

- wherever possible pair yellow to buff. If in doubt, pair to a clear buff mate with poor colour. Since the white has finer feathers you are more likely to get away with a double buff pairing if one partner is white.
- there is no sex linkage as there is with cinnamons. You need a white parent of either sex to produce whites, which in turn could be of either sex. There are no hidden carriers.
- never pair white to white if you wish to retain type and cobbiness.
- old-fashioned fanciers will advise you not to use normal birds produced from a mating where one parent is white as it will spoil the colour. I think this is nonsense. However, if you do, use poor coloured birds to mate with whites, so that it is that poor colour you will carry back, not the effect of the white.

Blue Fifes

These are simply the self Fifes in a white ground bird. Similarly, variegated white ground Fifes will be blue and white.

For exhibition purposes the blue should be a rich blue colour and level throughout, free from brown or yellow tints (buttercup influence) and have fine pencilling in the self birds.

Fawn Fifes

Fawn Fifes are white ground birds (white through to blue) but carry the cinnamon chromosome so are cinnamon rather than green feathered. The colour is normally achieved by pairing a cinnamon cock bird to a white hen – that way you are almost certain of producing fawn hens. If this pairing is not available then a cinnamon carrier to a white hen will produce the odd fawn hen. This is because cinnamon is sex-linked and white is not.

You cannot produce a fawn Fife without using a cock bird that either is cinnamon or carries the cinnamon gene.

For exhibition purposes the colour should be a level, rich fawn colour throughout, free from light areas and yellow feathers. The markings should be fine and a darker fawn as in the cinnamons.

On a variegated fawn Fife the white will be whiter than on a blue and white as the fawn is a cinnamon and the black pigment has been taken out of the white feathering as well as out of the green feathering.

The simplest method of producing fawns is to pair a well feathered cinnamon cock to a white hen. That way you can identify exactly what genes the youngsters carry. The preferred method to retain type, cobbiness and quality is probably the cinnamon carrier to a white hen.

The cinnamon cock x white hen produces:

- 25% white ground cocks (cinnamon carrier)
- 25% cinnamon carrier normal cocks
- 25% cinnamon hens
- 25% fawn hens

The cinnamon carrier x white hen produces:

- $12^1/2$% normal cocks
- $12^1/2$% normal cocks (cinnamon carriers)
- $12^1/2$% white ground cocks
- $12^1/2$% white ground cocks (cinnamon carriers)
- 25% normal hens
- 25% white ground hens

In the second year following the cinnamon cock x white ground hen pairing, white ground cinnamon carrier cocks can be paired to cinnamon hens. This will produce:

- $12^1/2$% cinnamon cocks
- $12^1/2$% fawn cocks
- $12^1/2$% normal cocks (cinnamon carriers)
- $12^1/2$% white cocks
- $12^1/2$% cinnamon hens
- $12^1/2$% fawn hens
- $12^1/2$% normal hens
- $12^1/2$% white hens

The fawn cocks from these matings are very useful as a foundation for white ground and cinnamon birds as they are capable of producing fawn, cinnamon, normal and white ground hens from one mating.

Such a bird is best paired to a normal hen with plenty of feather as the repeated matings of white and cinnamon tends to fine down the feather, which may result in youngsters with poor heads.

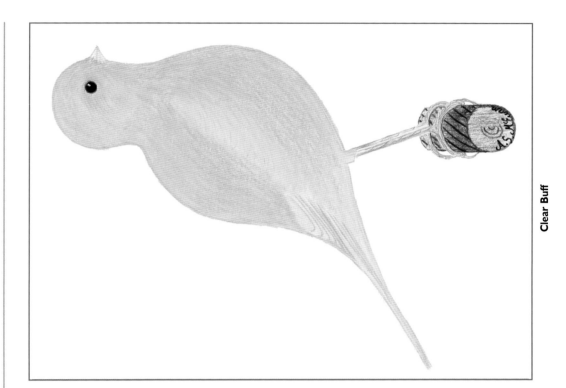

Clear Buff

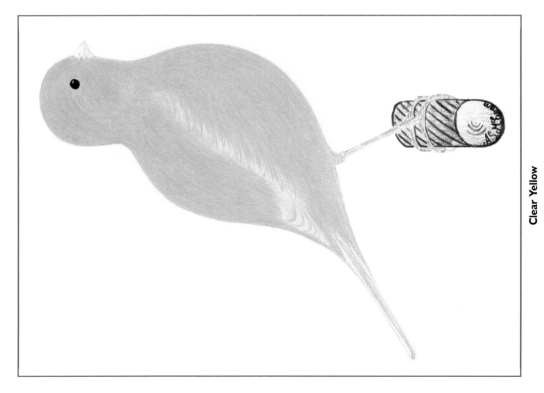

Clear Yellow

Variegated Yellow

Variegated Yellow

Heavy Variegated Yellow

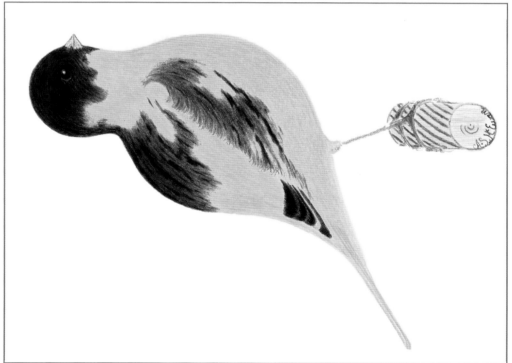

Variegated Yellow

Variegated Buff

Variegated Buff

Three Part Dark Buff

Heavy Variegated Buff

Self Green Buff

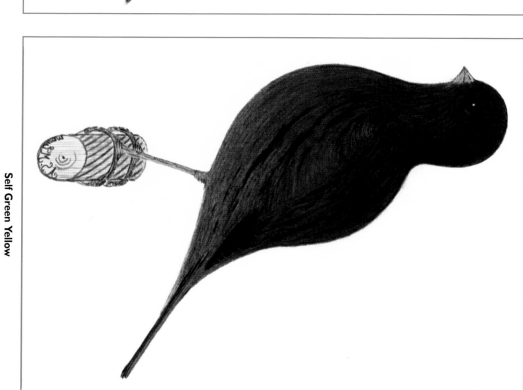

Self Green Yellow

Self Cinnamon Buff

Self Cinnamon Yellow

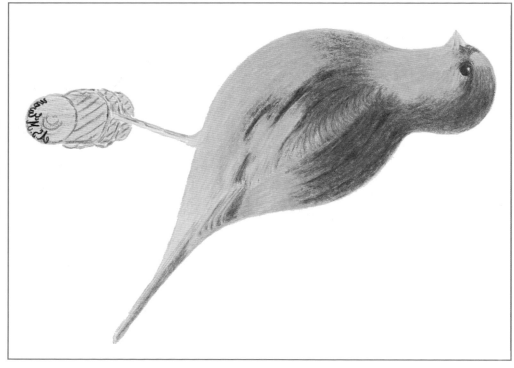

Variegated Yellow Cinnamon

Variegated Yellow Cinnamon

Variegated White

Variegated White

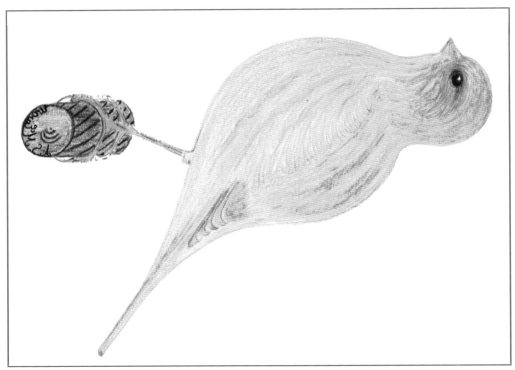

Fawn Self

Blue Self

Chapter
Twelve Month by Month

December

For me the year starts the first week in December when I return home with my show team from the National Exhibition Centre and place them in the flight cages along with the other Fifes I am to retain.

All surplus birds should now have gone. Always retain two yellow and two buff hens as spares in case one dies over the winter or during breeding. This is particularly important if, like me, you retain one or two old hens because of their history and pedigree.

General management

This is the month for winding down after a hectic breeding and show season. Christmas is a good time to wash the breeding cages and partitions thoroughly with a mild disinfectant such as Vanodine. Also empty and wash all show cages and perches and put them away for another year.

Place the hens in the longest flights possible. If certain cages get early-morning sun then the priority should be to allow the old hens access to this. In a small stud it might be possible to house the cocks singly but I keep my 16 cocks together in one 2.4m (8ft) long flight. *In order to avoid territorial squabbles, do not keep just two or three cocks together.*

Offer baths once a week (more frequently if possible) and clean out the flights weekly. When replacing the sawdust sprinkle granulated charcoal and oystershell grit on to the floor.

This month the days continue to get shorter so the length of daylight should not be changed by artificial light. Set the thermostat at 7–10°C (45–50°F). Allow the birds plenty of fresh air but close the windows on very cold and damp nights.

Diet

We now need to start the slow process of preparing for next year's breeding season. Some of the show team might be a little overweight but once in the flights much of this will be lost. Keep the birds (particularly the hens) on a plain diet of 50% Plain Canary and 50% Haith's Deluxe or Super Canary.

Greenfood as described earlier is very important and I provide it daily throughout the year but broccoli and similar should be given at least every other day with apple once a week.

Give them the softfood mixture once a week but there is no need for condition seed this month.

If greenfood is not available, one of the proprietary iron and vitamin tonics should be added to the drinking water twice a week.

January

General maintenance

This is the worst month of the year for the aviculturalist as the activity is one of feeding and cleaning out and the breeding season seems to be so far away. This is when wooden nest pans can be made and linings can be sewn into the pans in preparation.

Continue to offer baths weekly, even in the coldest weather. Finish off washing and painting breeding cages. Increase the daylight *in the morning* by 10–15 minutes a week only.

Diet

Continue with the December diet but now add a little of my condition mixture and niger (no more than 10%) to the mixture. Niger, being a member of the thistle family, is a mild conditioner. Watch any Fife that chases other birds off the mixture and frantically eats the niger as it may be out of condition. Niger should be fed sparingly; it does not reduce the risk of egg-binding.

February

General management

Towards the end of the month I like to paint my breeding cages and partitions white and also spray the cage fronts black. This also gives an air of anticipation for the forthcoming breeding season.

Finalise the selection of your breeding pairs if not already done so. Towards the end of the month catch every Fife and spray its rump with Johnson's Anti-Mite and then sprinkle Johnson's Ridmite powder all over its back and wings. (I use these preparations but others are available.) When every bird has had this treatment hang a Vapona block in the centre of the birdroom. *This is the first step in a process that will ensure you never have mite in your birdroom.* Prevention is better than cure and I have had no trace of mite even in the hottest of summers for 20 years.

Increase the morning daylight by 15 minutes a week.

Diet

As January but feed a little more condition seed mixture in addition to basic seed diet.

March (first half)

General management

Two weeks after the Fifes have been given their anti-mite treatment repeat the process so that any mites that were incubating 2 weeks ago will be killed. Check for excess fat on any bird and put those birds on a plain diet with plenty of greenfood.

Continue with regular baths.

Place the cocks in single cages. Trim the back toe nail and middle front toe nail.

Extend the morning daylight for 15 minutes each week this month.

Diet

As February but increase the condition seed mixture slightly. Add a little wheat germ oil to the mixture and allow it to soak in overnight. Offer the hens additional cuttlefish bone or liquid calcium in the water. Collect early seeding coltsfoot and chickweed but feed sparingly. Dandelion leaves and roots cut down the middle also can be offered.

March (second half)

General management

Treat the unflighted hens for mite, trim their nails and place them in single cages if they appear fit. The older hens and those still overweight should be left in the flight cage until the middle of April and given an iron tonic for 10 days.

Plant perpetual spinach and African marigold seed for the summer.

Collect moss for nesting material but be careful to wash it thoroughly. At the end of the month artificial light can be discontinued.

Diet

As the first half of March but chickweed or early dandelions (leaf, roots and heads) can be provided quite regularly. Condition seed can be given more often at the expense of condition food but not in excess – a daily sprinkling is sufficient.

April

Breeding will now be well under way (see chapters 5 and 6).

General management

After the final clean-out of the hens' cages where eggs are set, cover the cage floor with cat litter, which is very absorbent. The cages can then be left until the young have been weaned before the next full clean-out.

Spray nest pan linings with anti-mite spray before placing them in breeding cages.

If outdoor aviaries are being used, the soil should be given a sprinkling of lime. Check the mesh for holes and paint it black before any birds are allowed access.

Offer the hens a weekly bath until they have laid a full clutch.

Diet

Feed chickweed and early seeding dandelions particularly to backward hens. Provide plenty of cuttle for the hens. Do not neglect the cocks; continue to feed them a little softfood and greenfood regularly, although the hens will now be sitting on eggs and only need a very plain seed diet.

May

General management

Remove the Vapona block a couple of days before the first young hatch.

At the third day after hatching run the cock back in the cage for half an hour if you are using pairs. After 5–6 days he can be left in to help the hen rear the youngsters without any trouble. When the young are 14–15 days old put a second pan in the cage and offer new nesting material. Clean out the hen's cage when the young are weaned and have been moved to training cages at 22–24 days. Offer her new cuttle and an iron tonic for a few days.

Diet

As April. Dandelion seeding heads will be plentiful and can be fed to cocks and hens alike, particularly the ones who are not in condition.

June

General management

Try to keep the birdroom as cool as possible in hot weather. Keep a close eye out for stale softfood.

Diet

Green seeding dock should be available in plenty for collection and feeding to the weaned youngsters in addition to the diet described in Chapter 7.

July

General management

This is the month to end breeding operations and concentrate on a quick, clean moult. Decide which adults you wish to keep so that you can determine what youngsters to select for breeding.

Diet

Continue to feed the chicks green seeding dock and seeding grasses in addition to the softfood and greenfood. Adults about to moult should be fed these additions regularly.

August

General management

Hang training cages on to the flights so that youngsters can run freely into them. Place the condition mixture in the water pots to encourage this.

Offer baths as often as possible.

Diet

Feed plenty of wildfood and greenfood this month with a few yellow African marigold flower heads.

Feed the hens that have stopped rearing an iron and vitamin tonic in the water for a few days.

September

General management

Start to train the first round youngsters. Place show birds in single cages and spray several times a week.

Continue to offer baths as often as possible to the remainder. Spray every bird with Johnson's Anti-Mite and Ridmite powder and hang a Vapona block in the birdroom until after the last show.

Sow black rape seed in grow bags for spring feeding.

Diet

Add sunflower oil to the seed mixture this month at the ratio of one litre bottle per 25kg (55lb) seed.

October

General management

Spray show birds every other day. Do not exhibit any Fife that appears off-colour as it could be ill and spread disease to other birds at the show. In my opinion any exhibitor who shows a sick bird should have all his birds withdrawn by the show manager to stop any possible cross infection.

Diet

Continue with basic diet. Some fanciers feed pinhead oatmeal to the Fifes to slow them down for showing but some birds are liable to put on weight if fed too liberally.

November

General Management

This month sees the main show season activity, particularly the Fife specialist shows. Wash the show cages and perches after every show and wipe the cage fronts with turpentine to give a nice finish.

Diet

As wildfoods are no longer available feed the softfood mixture at least once a week with regular greenfood from the supermarket.

Chapter
Thirteen Ailments and Parasites

Fifes are hardy and accommodating little birds and rarely fall ill if certain rules are applied.

Prevention

There is no doubt in my mind that a stud of Fife canaries kept in a shed outdoors will have more illnesses than a single Fife kept in a warm house.

Most illnesses in young and old Fifes are caused by poor husbandry or general maintenance and are digestive or respiratory.

It is far easier to adopt a prevention policy than to effect a cure. Sadly in a stud of Fifes, particularly where the owner is out at work for most of the day, by the time a sick bird is identified the symptoms have usually gone too far. Even if the bird then responds to treatment it will probably be of no further use in the breeding programme, particularly if it is a hen, as hens have to carry out most of the work.

The aim must always be to keep all your Fifes in tip-top condition at all times. As a general rule I lose 1% of weaned youngsters during the breeding season due to illness and I would expect to lose one or even two of the flighted birds over winter out of forty. These in the main will be birds aged 2–3 years.

Keeping a young stud

Modern stud canaries are not long lived. After three breeding seasons the hen Fifes I have kept for this length of period are killed humanely as it is unlikely they will rear successfully for a fourth or fifth breeding season. Cocks can go on for a couple of years longer.

In the early 1980s I had a hen Fife who had lived for 9 years and reared for 7 of them. As she was the founder of my best stud I didn't have the heart to kill her and in those days Fifes – and other breeds of canaries – seemed to go on for much longer.

Do not take your old birds to the local pet shop. This is totally unfair. Children usually purchase their first canaries from a pet shop unless a member of their family is in the hobby. That youngster has no chance of breeding from old stock in his or her first breeding season and will be lost to the hobby.

The 3-year rule is necessary in an established stud. However, several years ago I gave my gardener a cock Fife which he kept in his living room near the television. In the late autumn he asked if I had a hen "for company for him". Although I tried to dissuade him I eventually gave him a 4-year-old hen that I would have killed anyway. That summer whilst rearing young chicks she had suddenly gone blind and lost part of several of her toes, although I got her sight back (dealt with under **Eye troubles/blindness** later on in the chapter).

I supplied my gardener with the usual nest pan and equipment and the following February the hen laid fertile eggs and reared the youngsters. That would not have been achieved in my birdroom in April. The warm living room and excessive light had put his pair into a high breeding condition many weeks before my own birds came into condition. This is an example that breaks the rules and raises the question of warmth for the well-being of canaries.

Older birds are liable to suffer from illnesses which is why, in a stud, fanciers are best working with young birds. In the 1920s the average lifespan for men was 56; today it is 20 years longer, but with that come additional diseases and illnesses. In Victorian days we had few heart problems, cancers and so on because we did not live long enough to get them! A young stud, particularly hens, makes Fife husbandry easier. An experienced fancier will show a novice how to kill old birds humanely.

Rules for good management

With poor management young birds will succumb to illnesses and diseases. To keep these to a minimum I would strongly recommend:

1   Fresh water at least every other day. Clean the drinkers out thoroughly and add Vanodine to the washing-up bowl. Some fanciers filter the birds' water and continental breeders purchase bottled water – I find this unnecessary.
2   Be very careful with additives to the drinking water, particularly yeast-forming ones such as glucose in summer. These days I do not add anything to the drinking water.
3   Always have plenty of good seed in the hoppers so that the Fifes will not go around picking up old food from the floor. Top up daily after blowing off the husks. When going on holiday make sure the birds have more than enough good seed. Some fanciers have winnowing machines to blow away husks and dirt from the seed. I prefer to empty the hoppers and throw the seed out for the wild Chaffinches and Greenfinches.
4   Fresh air should be the norm at all times, no matter how cold it is outside. You must avoid draughts, so ensure that no bird is near an open window in the cold weather.
5   Cleanliness is the key. Clean out cages of adults weekly including perches so that the floor stays clean and the Fifes do not get excrement on their feet or pick up stale food.
6   Clean down the birdroom regularly so that germs cannot 'hide'. This is the only problem with using ionisers – they keep the air clean but the dust has to go somewhere and it ends up on the walls and the back of the cages.
7   Give fresh greenfood and apple regularly – the adage *an apple a day keeps the doctor away* works just as well for Fifes!

Medicine cupboard

Sooner or later a Fife will become sick and I would advise you to buy the following for such emergencies and also for prevention:

- Antibiotics from the vet – I prefer Terramycin but Auronyin or Sulphamezathene are similar
- Bottle of TCP
- 5ml syringe from the chemist
- Syrup of buckthorn
- Kaolin powder
- Iron and vitamin tonic (liquid) or Abidec
- Johnson's Anti-mite spray or similar
- Johnson's Ridmite powder or similar
- Vapona block or similar
- Aloe Vera gel

NB Not Epsom salts, which can be too strong for a Fife.

Isolation

Once a sick Fife is spotted (usually fluffed up or with wings down and eyes not fully open) it must be removed from the other birds immediately. A good time to check on a stud when in flight cages is an hour or so before roosting when an unfit bird will go to roost sooner than normal and will often roost on the floor.

It is vital to reduce the bird's stress by placing it in a single cage way from the other birds. Prior to this, as soon as I am about to catch the bird, I mix a concentrated drop of Terramycin which I then insert into the Fife by using a plastic 5ml syringe.

Once isolated most birds will benefit from some form of heat. Purpose-made hospital cages are available but I do not like them as I feel the bird is placed under more stress in such a small environment with a glass front. Many fanciers use them but, in the old days, they would place a bird in the airing cupboard in a familiar training cage. I still prefer this method, as the bird will go to roost and therefore has rest, antibiotics and heat. Central heating radiators in the house will no doubt serve the same purpose. Other fanciers like to keep the bird in a breeding cage and place a lamp focussed on the bird, thus providing heat while leaving the bird in its own environment so as not to create additional stress.

Diet

Finally, place the bird on a soft diet. Give no hard seed in case the problem is one of the digestive system – offer softfood and apple only.

To summarise:

1 Remove the birds away from others
2 Administer antibiotics
3 Reduce stress
4 Provide warmth
5 Provide a soft diet

No matter what the illness, these basic rules are essential.

Keep the Fife under these conditions for 6 days while adding antibiotics at the recommended dosage to the drinking water.

This treatment will cure 90% of curable bird ailments in 6 days. Most birds will then appear bright-eyed and fit and can be returned to the flight cage.

My own view (and I have discussed this with my vet who agrees entirely) is that the Fife has such small, sensitive organs that, if it contracts a disease, it will die or be cured quickly. By the time the disorder is spotted it is well advanced, as a Fife cannot tell you it has a temperature in the early stages. If a Fife is still ill after 2 weeks of this treatment it should be humanely killed. I have visited other fanciers who have had such birds in the house for weeks trying to cure them to no avail. Such birds are disastrous in a breeding programme.

Common complaints

These are the most common ailments, illnesses and accidents that a Fife fancier might encounter, particularly in older birds.

Enteritis

This is often referred to as 'going light' in young birds as they tend to waste away despite appearing to eat off the floor all the time. Any bird on which I have had a post mortem carried out over the past 30 years has been identified as dying from this. Follow the instructions described earlier but react quickly.

Diarrhoea/constipation

Both should be rare if the bird is given a good diet. Place the bird in a training cage with kitchen roll on the floor to identify any digestive problems. If the droppings are very watery then administer a little light Kaolin powder. The old-time fanciers used to swear by syrup of buckthorn. For constipation (more common in winter) offer greenfood and place the bird in a warm environment.

Broken leg

An extra pair of hands is required to apply a splint such as a matchstick which can be held in place with strong sellotape. This may need replacing after a bath. After a couple of weeks the break should be well on its way to being mended. Be very careful when removing the splint.

Eye troubles/blindness

Some birds appear to have a problem with one eye and continuously rub the eye on the perch and lose feathers around it. Keep the perches clean, isolate the bird, apply diluted TCP to the infected eye and offer antibiotics for 6 days. Several years ago one of my old hen Fifes suddenly went blind whilst she had youngsters in the nest but after several days of this treatment she regained her sight.

Strokes

Old birds are more liable to have strokes. They appear to be paralysed on one side and are unable to perch. Like humans they vary in intensity. Many will die or need to be killed humanely; others recover quickly and carry on as normal for a year or so.

Baldness
Usually this is due to a vitamin deficiency. Put an iron and vitamin tonic or aloe vera gel in the water.

Ring damage
Occasionally a bird will get its ring caught on a branch if kept in an outdoor aviary, or an old bird's leg scales will grow so that they grow over the ring. Check there is free movement of the ring each time the bird is powdered. One cinnamon cock I had 20 years ago lost a foot this way but still managed to mate and fertilise eggs. If the ring has become stuck with age gently open it by using the tool supplied by the ring makers for putting it on.

Long nails have also a habit of getting caught if not checked, so cut them back each year.

False moult
Occasionally some Fifes, usually the clear birds, will go into a false moult. Each time this has been due to change in temperature such as a show hall that was too warm.

Disorders of rearing hens
The amount of work they carry out (swallowing droppings until the young are several days old, egg laying and so on) will affect a hen who is not fully fit. Some years ago several top fanciers lost several of their hens between the first and second rounds. This was a mystery for some time but it was eventually diagnosed as E coli peritonitis. If many hens die at this stage (you will always lose the odd one) then consult your vet with this information.

Sweating hens
This is a condition from which hens with chicks suffer very occasionally when the chicks have not been reared correctly. See Chapter 6.

Parasites
All wild birds carry insect parasites as these breed on the bird and then move on to the young in the nest. In the main, mites such as red or northern appear to be the most common. Prevention as described in Chapter 12 should be foolproof but if your Fifes go to a show and come into contact with other birds they may carry a few back.

At this time of year a Vapona block, or two in a large birdroom, placed strategically should kill these off before they can get established.

Some old fanciers and books will say that mite is carried into the birdroom on chickweed. This is absolute nonsense as the mites live on blood. Fodder mite in the cage that, when present, congregate under the chickweed (attracted by the moisture) may have caused this confusion. These are harmless to birds but should nevertheless be kept down by regular cleaning.

As a final deterrent against red mite, spray all your cages with Duranitex at the recommended dose. Some fanciers soak their nest linings in this product just prior to the breeding season. It is an excellent insect killer, used by leading pigeon fanciers.

Conclusion
I have resisted the temptation to provide an endless list of avicultural diseases ranging from canary pox to avian tuberculosis as during the past 40 years of breeding British birds and canaries I have never knowingly experienced any of them. To provide such a list would also lead the reader to think keeping canaries is far more difficult than it is.

If a bird does fall ill then isolate it quickly, treat it with antibiotics and keep it warm. That is all the newcomer or indeed an experienced fancier needs to know.

Keeping Fifes, or any other type of bird, is a wonderful, enjoyable and rewarding hobby. Look after your Fifes as you would look after your children; set high standards of cleanliness and give them clean water, good seed and a few extras. If that is too much to ask then consider another hobby which does not involve livestock.

Useful Addresses
Specialist Club List

North of England FFCC
Secretary: Mr A Dean
1 Scawthorpe Place
Pontefract
West Yorkshire   WF8 2HT

Fife Fancy Canary Club (FFCC)
Secretary: Mr A McEwan
'Emah Roo', 6 Forbes Street
Alloa
Clackmannanshire   FK10 1NF
Tel: 01259 213997

FFCC of Wales
Secretary: Mrs M James
8 Erw Wen
Llandulas, Abergele
Clwyd   LL22 8JN
Tel: 01492 515160

East Anglian FFCC
Secretary: Mr C Wilding
5 Oliver Place
The Grove
Essex   CM4 2UD
Tel: 01376 514370

London and South FFCC
Secretary: Mr D Day
11 Adelaide Gardens
South Benfleet
Essex   SS7 1LA
Tel: 01286 752501

Tyne Tees FFCC
Secretary: Mr R Jack
12 Queen Street
Grange Villa
Chester Le Street
Durham   DH2 3LT
Tel: 01913 701394

Southern England Fife Club
Secretary: Mr P Gray
45 Ackerman Street
Eaton Socon
Cambs
Tel: 01480 380147

International Fancy Fife Canary
Association
Secretary: Mr C Harris
32 Brentwood Road
Headington
Oxford   OX3 9LF
Tel: 01865 762505

Shropshire, Salop & District FFCC
Secretary: Mr T Armstrong
20 Riddings Close
Ketley, Telford
Shropshire   TF1 4HG
Tel: 01952 612446

Kent and Sussex FFCC
Secretary: Mr S Stafford
3 Chilton Lane
Ramsgate
Kent   CY1 1LG

Lanarkshire and Lothian FFCC
Secretary: Mr John Kelly
42 Balloch Road
Dykehead
Shotts   ML7 4HL

Terry Kelly
'Woollendale'
Cop-royd
Honley
Huddersfield   HD7 2LH
e-mail: Terry@tkpl.demon.co.uk

GC & WFFCC
Secretary: Mr R A Jones
10 Cherry Tree Drive
St Martin's (Nr Oswestry)
Shropshire   SY11 3QG
Tel: 01691 774361

Southern Counties FC
Secretary: Mrs H Emery
8 Kipling Road
Eastleigh
Hants   SO50 9EG
Tel: 023 8061 6081

West of Scotland FFCC
Secretary: Mr W McKay
43 Drysdale Avenue
Whitburn
West Lothian   EH47 0HW
Tel: 01501 741569

West Wales FFCC
Secretary: Mr D Griffiths
Croesyceillog Fach Cottage
Croesyceillog
Carmarthen   Dyfed   SA32 8DP
Tel: 01267 232033

North West FFCC
Secretary: Mr G Ackerley
91 Blaguegate
Lathom
Skelmersdale
Tel: 01695 732995

Dutch FFCC
H J Snoeren
Jan V. Eyckhof 3
4907 MA Oosterhout
Holland
Tel: 0162 426682

Index